Responding to Emergencies and Fostering Development

The Dilemmas of Humanitarian Aid

EDITED BY

Claire Pirotte
Bernard Husson
François Grunewald

TRANSLATED BY
Julia Monod-Robinson

Zed Books
London and New York

Responding to Emergencies and Fostering Development: the Dilemmas of Humanitarian Aid
was first published in 1999 by
Zed Books Ltd, 7 Cynthia Street, London N1 9JF, UK and
Room 400, 175 Fifth Avenue, New York, NY 10010, USA

Distributed in the USA exclusively by St Martin's Press, Inc.,
175 Fifth Avenue, New York, NY 10010, USA.

Published with support of the International Committee of the Red Cross.

Cover design by Andrew Corbett
Set in 10½/12 pt Berkeley Book
by Long House, Cumbria, UK
Printed and bound in the United Kingdom
by Biddles Ltd, Guildford and King's Lynn

A catalogue record for this book
is available from the British Library

US CIP has been applied for

ISBN   Hb 1 85649 754 2
       Pb 1 85649 755 0

Contents

Acronyms and Abbreviations

ACF	Action contre la faim
ACORD	Agency for Cooperation and Research in Development
ANS	Action Nord Sud
ASI	Acteurs de la solidarité internationale
AVICEN	Aide et Action
BHR	Bureau of Humanitarian Response
CCFD	Comité catholique contre la faim et pour le développement
CCL	Comité de coopération avec le Laos
CFCF	Comité français contre la faim
CFSI	Comité français de solidarité internationale
CICDA	Centre international de coopération pour le développement agricole
CIEDEL	Centre international d'études pour le développement local
CIEPAC	Centre international pour l'éducation permanente et l'aménagement concerté
CIMIC	Civil Military Cooperation
CIRAD	Centre internationale de recherche agronomique pour le développement
CLONGD	Comité de liaison des organisations non-gouvernementales de développement
COTA	Comité pour les technologies appropriées
DG VIII	Directorate General VIII, the European Union
DTA	District Transition Assembly
ECHO	European Commission on Humanitarian Operations
ECOSOC	(UN) Economic and Social Commission
EDF	European Development Fund
FAO	Food and Agriculture Organisation
FEWS	Famine Early Warning System
FFW	Food for Work
GRDR	Groupe de recherche et de réalisation pour le développement rural dans le Tiers Mode
GRET	Groupe de recherche et d'échanges technologiques
HI	Handicap International
ICRC	International Committee of the Red Cross
ICVA	International Commission of the Voluntary Agencies
IDP	Internally displaced person
IEDES	Institut d'études de développement
IFOR	International Force for Bosnia Herzegovina
IMF	International Monetary Fund

IRAM	Institut de recherche et d'applications des méthodes de développement
IRIS	Institut des relations internationales et stratégiques
IUED	Institut universitaire des études de développement
LDC	Local development committee
MCC	Mother and child care
MDM	Médecins du Monde
MSF	Médecins sans frontières
MSL	Mouvement social libanais (Lebanese Social Movement)
MST	Mobile support team
NATO	North Atlantic Treaty Organisation
NGO	Nongovernmental organisation
OAP	Operation d'appui à l'autopromotion
OAU	Organisation of African Unity
ODA	Overseas Development Assistance
OECD	Organisation for Economic Cooperation and Development
OXFAM	Oxford Committee for Famine Relief
PHARE	Aid for the Economic Reconstruction of Poland and Hungary
RDP	Popular Democratic Republic
RPF	Rwandan Popular Forces
SADC	Southern African Development Community
SAMU	Secours et assistance médicale d'urgence
SFOR	Special Force for Bosnia Herzegovina
SIDKA	Syndicate for the management of farming lands
SOLAGRAL	Solidarités agricoles et alimentaires
SP	Shining Path
TACIS	Technical Assistance to the Community of Independent States
UN	United Nations
UNAVEM	United Nations Mission for the Verification of Ceasefire in Angola
UNDP	United Nations Development Program
UNHCR	United Nations High Commissioner for Refugees
UNICEF	United Nations Children's Fund
UNTAC	United Nations Transitional Authority for Cambodia
URD	Urgence–Réhabilitation–Développement
USAID	US Agency for International Development
VOICE	Voluntary Organisation for Cooperation in Emergencies
VSF	Vétérinaires sans frontières
WFP	World Food Programme

List of Contributors

Valérie Belchior-Bellino, Action contre la faim (ACF)

Hervé Bernard, Action Nord Sud (ANS)

Jean-Eudes Beuret, Centre international de coopération pour le développement agricole (CICDA)

Philippe Biberson, interview, Médecins sans frontières, France (MSF-F)

Judy El Bushra, Agency for Cooperation and Research in Development (ACORD)

Eliane Comatri-Mitri, Mouvement social libanais (MSL)

Bérengère Cornet-Vernay, Comité catholique contre la faim et pour le développement (CCFD)

Annette Corrèze, Centre international d'études pour le développement local (CIEDEL)

Mark Duffield, Institute of Development Studies, Sussex University, UK

Carlo von Flüe, International Committee of the Red Cross (ICRC)

Christian Fusillier, Institut de recherches et d'applications des méthodes de développement (IRAM)

François Grunewald, President, Urgence–Réhabilitation–Développement (URD) Group, former international development consultant, ICRC

Geneviève Guillou (ANS)

Bill Howell, Handicap International (HI)

Bernard Husson (CIEDEL), former Director General of Comité français de solidarité internationale(CFSI)

Yannick Lassica, Centre international pour l'éducation permanente et l'aménagement concerté (CIEPAC)

Pierre Laurent, Médecins du Monde (MDM)

Philippe Leborgne (ACF)

Sylvie Mantrant, Voluntary Organisation for Cooperation in Emergencies (VOICE)

André Marty (IRAM)

Jacques Mercoiret (CIEPAC)

Xavier Ortégat (VOICE)

Richard Pinder, Equilibre

Claire Pirotte, coordinator of the URD-CIEDEL network

Bruno Rebelle, international development consultant, former director of VSF (Vétérinaires sans frontières)

Jean-Baptiste Richardier (HI)

Marc Rodriguez, Groupe de recherches et d'échanges technologiques (GRET)

Jean-Christophe Ruffin, Institut des relations internationales et stratégiques (IRIS)

Claude Simonot (HI)

Marie-Cecile Thirion, Solidarités agricoles et alimentaires (SOLAGRAL)

Philippe Truze, Aide et Action (AVICEN)

Pascal Vincent (CIEDEL)

Members of the
Urgence–Réhabilitation–Développement (URD) Group

Action contre la faim (ACF)
Agence de coopération technique pour le développement (ACTED)
Amnesty International, France (observer status)
Bioforce Catholic Relief Services and CARITAS CARE, France
Centre international de coopération pour le développement agricole (CICDA)
Centre international d'études pour le développement local (CIEDEL)
Comité catholique contre la faim et pour le développement (CCFD)
Coordination SUD
Pierre de Montaigne, Institute of Technology, University of Bordeaux
Professor M. J. Domestici, University of Aix en Provence
Glob-action
Groupe de recherche et d'échanges technologiques (GRET)
Groupe de recherche et de réalisation pour le développement rural dans le Tiers
   Monde (GRDR)
Professor André Gschaoua, University of Lille
Hôpital sans frontières (HSF)
Institut de formation pour l'action international en développement (IFAID)
Institut de recherches et d'applications des méthodes de développement (IRAM)
Institut universitaire des études de développement (IUED)
International Committee of the Red Cross (ICRC) (observer status)
Médecins du Monde (MDM)
Médecins sans frontières (MSF)
Overseas Development Institute (ODI)
Partage
Pharmacien sans frontières (PSF)
Professor Philippe Ryfman, University of Paris/Sorbonne
Solidarités agricoles et alimentaires (SOLAGRAL)
Vétérinaires sans frontières
Voluntary Organisation for Cooperation in Emergencies (VOICE)

Preface

Luc Paunier

President, Geneva Foundation for Health in War

In recent years both the nature and the duration of armed conflicts have changed considerably. The increasingly frequent and systematic targeting of civilian populations and of their life-support systems gives rise to a number of very diverse problems for which there are no easy solutions. The problem is further complicated by the fact that experience gained in one type of situation is not necessarily applicable elsewhere, for reasons such as cultural differences between the targeted populations or different topographical and climatic conditions – not to mention the overriding security factor. The growing number of low intensity conflicts poses the problem of their duration, which is no doubt one of the main reasons for the research into the relationships between emergency, rehabilitation and development that gave rise to this book. The approach adopted by the Urgence–Réhabilitation–Développement (URD) Group has the merit of calling into question practices that are not necessarily suited to relief actions in this new context, insofar as they do not allow the affected populations to resume a normal life and reclaim their independence. It is to be hoped that these questions, which have been a major concern of many humanitarian agencies for several years, will be answered with practicable solutions that meet the needs of the victims while at the same time avoiding the trap of oversimplification. Because of the importance of this debate, the Geneva Foundation felt it worthwhile to finance the translation of this book, which addresses a very topical theme. Special thanks are due to Julia Monod-Robinson who has produced a faithful and fluid translation that demonstrates a fine understanding of this complex subject.

Foreword

JOANNA MACRAE

Humanitarian Policy Group
Overseas Development Institute

It is no coincidence that the last war in Europe in this millennium has been called a humanitarian war. The full implications and meaning of the NATO intervention in Kosovo in the spring of 1999 have yet to be understood. What it made clear, however, was that the humanitarian agenda is no longer always on the margins of aid and political debates – rather, it is sometimes at the centre. How to respond to massive violations of human rights and humanitarian law by state and non-state actors is now a major question for international relations.

The 1990s saw a rapid expansion in the value and volume of relief, once the orphan of official aid. In 1980 the value of relief aid (excluding food aid) from OECD countries was US$680 million. By 1996 this value had increased nearly fourfold to US$2.7 billion (OECD, various years). The rapid increase in the value of relief aid reflected not only increased need, but also the increased reach of the humanitarian system. As Duffield (1994) points out, until the mid-1980s relief was confined largely to the periphery of conflict – to safe government-held areas, and to the refugee camps in second countries to which large sections of conflict-affected populations fled. The important exception was, of course, the International Committee of the Red Cross (ICRC), which since its founding has always worked in conflict zones.

The slow thawing of the Cold War changed this. Access to civilians living in war zones expanded. At first this was through NGOs, particularly those linked to rebel movements such as the Eritrean Relief Association and Relief Society of Tigray (Duffield and Prendergast, 1994; Borton, 1994), both of which delivered relief cross-border to those living in rebel-held territory without the consent of the Ethiopian government. According to international law such an intervention was illegal. As the decade progressed, so NGOs and the UN started to negotiate access to conflict zones. Operation Lifeline Sudan, established in 1989, was the first attempt to institutionalise a framework to secure access to civilians on both (or later multiple) sides of the conflict.

During the 1990s the international community, or at least the Western donor governments, conducted a series of 'humanitarian experiments'. These sought largely to address the question of expanding humanitarian space, first through negotiation and, in some cases such as Iraq, Somalia and Bosnia, through force. The rationale, however, was to increase the delivery of relief goods, not to address the causes of the humanitarian crisis – in other words the crisis of protection (Tomasevski, 1994). If the limitations of such an approach needed to be proved, the genocide in Rwanda in 1994 did so.

The world stood by while one of the most efficient killing machines of the twentieth century did its work. In contrast with the sloth of the international political response, the humanitarian response to the aftermath of the genocide was considerable – an estimated US$1.4 billion in the period April–December 1994 alone (Eriksson, 1996). Much of this aid was delivered to the crowded camps along what was then the Zaïrean border with Rwanda. It was to these very camps that the organisers and perpetrators of the genocide had fled, dragging with them whole sections of the Hutu population. Within the camps these leaders, armed and organised, constituted a threat not only to the new government in Rwanda, but to the populations in the camps themselves. It was not long, therefore, before those who were delivering aid to the refugees were transformed by the media from white knights into demons – aid, it was said, was feeding the killers.

The Rwandan case exemplifies the fact that the increase of humanitarian space has brought with it a new wave of dilemmas, particularly for international NGOs. This book reflects the struggle within the humanitarian community to come to grips with working in complex political emergencies. It is a unique record of a process of discussion and debate between a group of French NGOs which has been working together for nearly five years to grapple with the conceptual and operational demands of working in these environments.

What is at issue is not primarily how to respond to the acute phase of these crises – the sudden refugee influxes, for example. Rather, what is of concern is that the aid community lacks the tools to respond to the needs of populations who live in environments of *chronic* physical, political, economic and environmental insecurity. In these environments relief aid is not enough, yet development aid is usually withheld by official aid actors. This book explores how aid agencies have adapted to what is increasingly called this 'grey zone' of chronic political emergencies.

The different chapters speak for themselves. This foreword aims to map out the common concerns emerging within the community, including those represented in this volume, and to identify areas where consensus remains elusive.

Some common concerns

Like the humanitarian system itself, in recent years the arena of humanitarian debate and research has been almost dizzying in its pace, breadth and volume. Five years ago it would have been difficult to discern many common threads in the array of conferences, books, papers and field documents emerging from the many humanitarian theatres, including those of aid agencies. As the system has matured, so the terms and issues of debate have become sharpened and there is a greater consensus on what the problems are. This book reflects five of the key concerns which straddle the humanitarian community, the factors which constitute what Pierre Laurent (pages 27–9) has called the humanitarian impasse.

First, there has been an explicit recognition of the inherently political nature of humanitarian action in war time. As Grunewald and Rodriquez ask in their introduction to Part III, 'Humanitarian intervention is confronted with the violence of politics. How to act, or not to act, under such conditions?' (page 68). This brings with it an acknowledgement that aid actors need to be politically informed in order to ensure that aid does not become incorporated into the conflict dynamics. As Yannick Lassica (page 134) points out with reference to Burundi, generating an accurate analysis of the political context is a prerequisite for effective and legitimate aid interventions. The difficulty of arriving at such an analysis is not underrated, however, given the continued validity of the old cliché that truth is war's first casualty.

A second concern reflected here is how to ensure the legitimacy and accountability of aid interventions in conflict-affected countries. However flawed in practice, traditionally the accountability of international aid has rested on the idea that the recipient state would sanction and monitor aid flows. Indeed this remains the norm for development-aid relations. How then to deal with what Robert Jackson (1990) has called 'quasi-states'? In such countries a central government does not exist (for example, Somalia); or the regime is not recognised as the legitimate authority by the international community (for example, Cambodia from 1982 to 1991); or the state's human rights abuses at home, or its behaviour towards third countries, renders it an international pariah (for example, Sudan, Serbia, Iraq).

The lack of a clear framework of governance has important implications for the way in which aid functions. If governments are not regulating the quality, distribution and volume of aid flows, who is? For example, in these stateless situations, who should decide where scarce resources should go, how they should be distributed to ensure equitable and efficient coverage? The contributions in this volume suggest how NGOs might work with 'fragments' of states, in particular the professional and technical components of public administrations. So, for example, Phillipe Truze (pages 137–43) describes how one NGO sought to bolster the capacity of the Ministry of Health in Afghanistan, so seeking to provide a mechanism to sustain national capacity for health planning and response. Similarly, André Marty (pages 39–41) describes how in North Mali agencies worked to support the establishment of interim authorities at the district level to provide a basis for public policy in the transitional period after the ending of the war in 1992. These types of initiative are one important response to the crisis of governance facing aid in conflict-affected countries. They are an attempt to respond to what Richardier (pages 26–7) in this volume and de Waal (1996, 1997) have identified as the risk that external interventions will weaken still further the fragile political relationship between the state (and non-state entities) and the populations living under their control. Of course, the difficulty is who should do what when existing political authorities fail systematically to demonstrate their concern for public welfare.

A third theme of current debates is the strain placed on the concepts of neutrality and impartiality in responding to complex political emergencies. The concept of neutrality implies not taking a political position in relation to the conflict, about who is right and who is wrong. That of impartiality states that relief goods should be distributed solely on the basis of need, not on the basis of political or religious affiliation, ethnicity or gender. These principles, which have their roots in operational pragmatism as well as a particular ethical tradition, are now questioned by some agencies and in some environments. Thus, for example, ACORD (pages 132–3) describes how, in the aftermath of the genocide, it concluded that a strictly neutral approach to its work in Rwanda would be unethical. Its analysis suggested that a ceasefire between the government and the RPF would have resulted in further massacres, and that in the medium term an RPF victory would yield a better human rights environment. This tension between solidarity and neutrality is a recurrent theme of current debates.

A fourth challenge is how to adapt to the chronic nature of complex political emergencies. This is not a new problem – wars were always long, and struggles in Eritrea, Mozambique and Angola, to name only a few, have lasted decades rather than years or months. What is new is a questioning of whether the existing tools to respond to conflict, and specifically *in* conflict situations, are appropriate to the task. This is the central question of this book and indeed of the Urgence–Réhabilitation–Développement Group (URD).

Relief aid traditionally provides material goods, such as food and medicines, to enable people to survive temporary crises. The classic relief model has its roots in responses to natural disasters such as floods and drought, the aim being to allow populations to survive until they can restore normal production. In conflict situations the problem is a different one. Interruptions to social and productive systems are not simply 'acts of god'; they are an intentional and central part of the strategy of war. Furthermore, the long duration of conflicts and the chronic nature of conflict-induced vulnerability are such that the 'band aid' approach is now widely questioned.

Now one hears increasingly loud calls for relief to be developmental, in other words for it to enable populations to reactivate their own strategies for survival, becoming independent and reducing their vulnerability to future hazards. This links with the fifth and final common theme of current humanitarian debate reflected in this book: that, as aid may fuel conflict, so it may be used to reduce tensions and as an instrument for conflict management. This approach draws significantly on an analysis of the political economy of war and a recognition of the possible incorporation of aid into a conflict dynamic, a theme touched on above. In their contributions, Ruffin (Chapter 3), Duffield (Chapter 5) and Grunewald (Chapter 7) describe the conflict dynamic and its political economy. Transforming aid from serving a purely palliative function to being part of a process of peace building is a significant step. It is one which is highlighted in this book (see, for example, Beuret, pages 120–1) and elsewhere (Anderson, 1996; European Commission, 1996; Development Assistance Committee, 1997).

An emerging (dis)sensus?

Part IV of the book is called 'Open Debates'. It reflects the fact that, in common with the wider international debate, while there is increasing agreement on the nature of the problem, solutions remain contentious. This should not be surprising, nor necessarily a difficulty. The complexity of the issues means that any claim to a monopoly of wisdom should be treated with extreme caution. As the book makes clear, no consensus on often contentious matters has been achieved even among the contributors to the URD process.

Grunewald's plea for a 'revolution' in the design of aid in wartime is undoubtedly shared by many, and the principles and practice which have guided relief action have been subject to new scrutiny and are prompting diverse and sometimes divisive responses. As it is possible to cluster common concerns, so it is possible to identify a number of key points of disagreement with regard to proposed solutions. These issues are likely to dominate humanitarian debates in coming years.

Standards or standardisation?

One response to the mounting critique of relief action in recent years has been moves to define clearer ethical and technical standards to guide operations. One of these has been the SPHERE initiative.[1] The definition of standards is seen as part of a process of bridging the accountability gap in international humanitarian response. The SPHERE project (1998) outlines minimum standards in water supply and sanitation, nutrition, food aid, shelter and site planning, and health services, together with indicators by which performance can be judged.

In the introduction to the book, Grunewald describes the URD group's opposition to this process, arguing that:

> Certainly, the Group agrees that humanitarian actors must strive for quality – their credibility depends on it. But let us not be taken in by simplistic solutions, particularly the current fad of standards. Those proposed by the SPHERE project do not take into account the cultural diversity and changing nature of contexts and crises.... Standardisation and homogenisation may in the long-run kill the creativity that is so necessary to a world in constant change.... All strategies of standardisation lead to the risk of 'standardised thought'.

A particular concern of URD and of critics of SPHERE, many of them from the Francophone humanitarian community, has been that the definition of standards might be coopted by the donor community. They identify the risk that standards may be used as a stick with which to beat NGOs, diverting attention away from the wider failings of donor governments and those of warring parties to provide an environment which protects basic human rights to life and dignity.

It is this issue, perhaps alone of those raised in the book, which suggests a strong distinction between Francophone and Anglo-Saxon traditions of humanitarian action. Their primary point of divergence is in the analysis of the relationship between international NGOs and the state. In the UK, USA and Scandinavia, NGOs often have a close, working relationship with their own governments, receiving a significant proportion of their budgets from official sources and having routine access to senior policy makers and politicians. In France the NGO community is much more sceptical of governmental action, fiercely guarding its independence from the state. One facet of this is an interpretation of the process of 'professionalisation' of aid, including humanitarian aid. While in Anglophone countries the term is used positively to denote competence and experience, in France it has become associated with the risk of institutionalising civil action and so losing the authenticity of international solidarity. Thus voluntarism remains a grounding principle in many French NGOs, particularly humanitarian NGOs.

On other issues, the differences of humanitarian opinion are less clearly demarcated along national lines. Rather, one can trace a number of schools of humanitarian thought defined across borders, but distinguished by organisational culture and philosophical tradition.

'Developmental relief': potential and limitations

Pivotal in the context of this book are questions regarding the extent to which aid actors working in conflict situations emphasise the delivery of relief on the basis of the values of traditional humanitarianism and political neutrality, or instead stress the developmental objective, designed to address conflict as the cause of the crisis.

This debate is at once conceptual, institutional and programmatic. At a conceptual level, those who advocate more developmental relief reject the distinction between relief and development aid as an artifact of aid history which has no place in current aid response to conflict (see, for example, El Bushra, pages 97–101). This view arises from an analysis taking the point of view of conflict-affected populations, for whom the reality of survival may differ little despite changes in the formal political and aid designations applied by international actors to different countries at different times. So, even in the middle of a conflict, there may be space for people to resume production, to learn new skills, to 'develop' and move out of a mode of passive receipt of relief goods.

Another approach is to view the distinction between relief and development aid as essentially political. This is in the sense of international political relations whereby bilateral donors, for example, withhold development aid on the grounds that they contest the legitimacy of the state in recipient countries. The scope to resume development aid is likely to be limited in situations where legitimacy remains contested. In other words the instruments for the delivery of relief aid remain highly decentralised, working largely outside public institutions and systems, and channelled through NGOs. While very important, such aid cannot influence structural factors such as macroeconomic policy or public health and education. From an aid perspective, in other words, while development aid is withheld, its developmental impact is necessarily limited to the micro level.

As the book points out, making aid more developmental – in the sense of trying to support national institutions, particularly civil institutions – requires great sensitivity and careful political analysis. Questions of which institutions should be strengthened are not straightforward in these complex political economies where it is difficult for organisations to remain 'above' or outside politics and militarism. At the same time, building alternative institutions to redress the balance against violent forces is clearly a priority. How to do this and who should do this are preoccupying and difficult questions, as Grunewald points out (pages 80–2).

Programming in practice

Finally, there is the question of what to do in these environments in programmatic terms. The book outlines a rich array of activities undertaken by different organisations from Afghanistan, Bosnia and Cambodia to what was formerly called Zaïre.

There is a consensus that rebuilding the infrastructure is not enough (see, for example, Rebelle, pages 35–9). However, the obstacles to developing more developmental approaches in these environments are formidable. Much is written of the limitations of existing relief-aid instruments, in terms of time frames (Simonot, pages 57–8; Guillou, pages 58–9) and the organisational culture of aid agencies (Guillou, pages 58–9; Grunewald, pages 54–5). The jury remains out, however, in terms of defining the extent and quality of developmental space in chronic political emergencies.

What the contributions in this volume suggest is that it is very difficult to generalise across settings. Within the book, as within the world, there is a notable diversity of need and of political context. There is a danger of failing to distinguish the difference between situations of post-conflict transition – such as those of Cambodia and Bosnia, where a political settlement, however flawed, was in place – and situations of ongoing violence, such as Sudan, Zaïre and Angola. Subsuming all unstable situations, regardless of their political status, under a generic 'instability', and assuming that within all of them development opportunities exist, is potentially problematic (see, special issue of *Disasters*, 22, 4).

While some see opportunities for political reform in wartime (see, for example, Rebelle pages 35–9; ACORD, pages 78–9), others are more cautious, arguing that, while there may be some room for developmental manoeuvre, this can be overstated in a context where for the majority life chances are deteriorating or at least remain very poor. In other words, there is the risk of seeming to normalise crisis, to rebrand it and relabel it as development (see, for example, Bradbury, 1998). Clearly it will be important to individual NGO project interventions to be seen within the overall context of political and economic circumstances, nation-wide.

Same landscapes, different maps

Any attempt to review the state of the art of contemporary humanitarianism, or at least a section of it, is confronted by the complexity of the problem and the increasing diversity of proposed solutions. In shedding the image that relief is merely an exercise in logistics, the humanitarian community has entered a new landscape. To navigate this landscape, road maps and trucks are not enough. Instead, those delivering relief in these complex environments are seeking to define a new rationale for their interventions, an ethic which can underpin efforts aimed at preventing and recovering from fires as well as putting them out.

What this book reflects is that while a universal humanitarian ethos in its broadest sense may unite those seeking to aid conflict-affected populations, the humanitarian stage is characterised by an increasingly disparate array of actors. These actors are interpreting their humanitarian obligations differently: some choose to reassert neutrality and impartiality, while others opt for solidarity; some focus on setting basic standards for the delivery of basic relief inputs, while others argue for a move away from things to institutions; some argue for a definition of universal standards, others adopt a more relativistic, culturally determined position; some argue for professionalisation, others resist the formalisation and institutionalisation of the humanitarian impulse;

some argue that aid can and should play a role in the management of conflict, others that to do so compromises its neutrality.

To a greater or lesser extent each of these different positions is explored in this book, and these tensions characterise humanitarian debate and practice more widely. Of course, what is of interest is not only how these debates play out on paper, but how they play out in practice. The methodological diversity (or anarchy to choose a more provocative term) which increasingly characterises aid agencies is perhaps preferable to a homogeneous application of humanitarian puritanism. However, a number of questions emerge from the current kaleidoscope of aid agencies in conflict situations:

First, from the point of view of belligerent parties, how will this diversity of approach be interpreted by warring parties and by intended beneficiaries? The United Nations' experience of pursuing multiple mandates – aid (relief and development), political and military – has not been happy (African Rights, 1994). Can an aid system in general, and NGOs in particular, convey to belligerent parties their own unique branding and objectives? What are the implications of the broadening and deepening of the humanitarian agenda (Leader, 1998) in terms of commitments by agencies and warring parties to initiatives such as Codes of Conduct and humanitarian principles established to regulate aid and war? If, on the one hand, some agencies are seeking to convince belligerents of their neutrality and impartiality in order to secure access, how is this affected when other agencies emphasise principles of solidarity?

A second issue is in relation to the management of bilateral aid. It is striking that a remarkably small group of Western donors contribute to official humanitarian aid flows. It is striking, too, that they continue to fund very diverse approaches to chronic political emergencies. While again not suggesting bland uniformity of planning approaches, questions are raised regarding the consistency of planning objectives. For example, is maintaining coverage of basic humanitarian inputs the priority, or is it outweighed by sustainability? Is the objective neutrality or institution building? Clarity is important not only for accountability but also for the design of aid instruments. At present it is easy to conclude that existing international relief instruments do not match increasingly diverse and complex objectives.

This book provides a rare snapshot of an ongoing debate. In addition to providing an insight into the thinking of a significant group of NGOs, it also helps to highlight and overcome the obstacles of language, organisational culture, and the schism which has divided relief and development aid actors. As such, it does not claim to provide answers. The URD process has sought to increase exchanges across the various lines – Anglophone–Francophone; academic–practitioner; humanitarian–developmental. In so doing it has drawn on and been informed by many different traditions, perhaps enabling them to become more mutually intelligible. Thus, this volume might contribute, if not to a consensus, then at least to greater understanding within the humanitarian community and between it and the rest of the world.

Note

1. SPHERE was initiated by the Steering Committee for Humanitarian Response Interaction, VOICE, the ICRC and ICVA.

References

African Rights (1994) *Humanitarianism Unbound?: Current Dilemmas Facing Multi-mandate Relief Operations in Political Emergencies*. Discussion Paper No: 5 . London: African Rights.

Anderson, M. (1996) *Do No Harm: Supporting Local Capacities for Peace through Aid*. Boston, MA: Collaborative for Development Action, Local Capacities for Peace Project.

Borton, J. (1994) *NGOs and Relief Operations: Trends and Policy Implications*. London: Overseas Development Institute.

Bradbury, M. (1998) 'Normalizing the Crisis in Africa'. *Disasters* 22, 328–38.

de Waal, A. (1996) 'Social Contract and Deterring Famine: First Thoughts'. *Disasters* 20: 194–205.

de Waal, A. (1997) *Famine Crimes: Politics and the Disaster Relief Industry in Africa*. Oxford: James Currey.

Development Assistance Committee (1997) *DAC Guidelines on Conflict, Peace and Development Cooperation*. Paris: OECD.

Duffield, M. (1994) 'Complex Emergencies and the Crisis of Developmentalism'. *IDS Bulletin* 25: 37–45.

Duffield, M. and Prendergast, J. (1994) *Without Troops and Tanks: Humanitarian Intervention in Ethiopia and Eritrea*. Lawrenceville: Red Sea Press.

Eriksson, J. (1996) *The International Response to Conflict and Genocide: Lessons from the Rwanda Experience*. Synthesis report, Copenhagen: Joint Evaluation of Emergency Assistance to Rwanda.

European Commission (1996). *Communication from the Commission to the Council and the European Parliament on Linking Relief, Rehabilitation and Development*. Brussels: European Commission.

Jackson, R. (1990) *Quasi-states: Sovereignly, International Relations and the Third World*. Cambridge: Cambridge University Press.

Leader, N. (1998) 'Proliferating Principles: How to Sup with the Devil Without Getting Eaten'. *Disasters* 22 (4): 288–308.

SPHERE (1998). *Humanitarian Charter and Minimum Standards in Disaster Response*. Geneva: the SPHERE Project.

Tomasevski, K. (1994) 'Human Rights and Wars of Starvation'. In: Macrae, J. and Zwi, A. (eds), *War and Hunger: Rethinking International Responses to Complex Emergencies*. London and New Jersey: Zed Books, pp. 70–91.

INTRODUCTION
In a Troubled World, We Must Remain Alert

FRANÇOIS GRUNEWALD
President of the URD Group

Ne laissez nulle place où la bêche ne passe et repasse
(*We must remain vigilant and constantly challenge
the findings of our analyses.*) – Jean de la Fontaine

The world has evolved at great speed since the fall of the Berlin Wall – how can we make our practices evolve to keep up with it? At the end of the 1980s, with that symbolic demolition and the fundamental changes that ensued, history went through a period of discontinuity. Some even pronounced it dead. The end of the Cold War represented a major break that became the reference date between the 'before' and the 'after'. The impact of this disruption on the history of the crisis-ridden planet also affected problems in the field, the way in which we interpret them and the activities to be undertaken.

It is in this context that the Urgence–Réhabilitation–Développement (URD) Group was born in 1993. A meeting point for the main French emergency and development NGOs, it soon welcomed other international solidarity groups and university institutes that were working towards the same goal. By collaborating with the International Committee of the Red Cross (ICRC), the Overseas Development Institute (ODI), the Agency for Cooperation and Research in Development (ACORD), as well as with the European collective, Voluntary Organisation for Cooperation in Emergencies (VOICE), the URD Group avoided an exclusively French outlook. The working method was based on free speech and non-institutional exchanges, and within that framework the URD Group launched its first major research studies. The findings of these studies were first discussed at an international symposium at the Arche de la Défense, Paris, in 1994. The operational research in the field (mainly in former Zaïre) and collective thematic analyses continued during the following years. The development agencies gradually became familiar with the crisis context, an approach that appeared all the more necessary as the number of countries for which a stable future could be forecast was dwindling: Kenya and Indonesia have joined the club of countries teetering on the brink of crisis, while Uganda – in spite of its good standing with the IMF – is once again taking the plunge. As for the emergency workers, they had to take into account – and integrate – longer time frames than those in which they normally operate. The findings of those four years have been comprehensively described in a collective work published in France in 1997. Now it is my pleasure to introduce this English-language edition.

The issues addressed in this book are many and cover areas of concern shared by many humanitarian groups: the relations between emergency and development groups; different types of emergency intervention and, particularly, the articulation between assistance and protection; and areas of synergy that can (or must) be established between food aid and strategies of support for survival, and between free aid and cost-recovery schemes.

New conflicts, old wars

The first phases of the thinking process led the URD Group to launch a study of war: it was necessary to acquire a better understanding of the new crises, contexts and field problems that were arising in the post-Cold War world, particularly in internal conflicts of a new kind. Internal conflicts – because we did not understand them – were described as 'destructured' conflicts. Only our short-sightedness led us to describe them thus. The Rwandan, Burundian, Somalian, and Sierra Leonean crises were in fact very structured. Unfortunately, we often lack the tools to decode these crises and analyse them. Indeed, what is one to do when not only does the military attack the civilian population, but civilians themselves attack other civilians? This phase was crucial to the collective task and to put into perspective the issues of prevention, disaster-preparedness, and the management and resolution of crisis.

Moreover, in the 'Post-Berlin Wall' ideology, international conflicts had almost been forgotten. The crisis areas of the world were thus reduced to a handful of places on the planet where ethnic groups (European, African or other) were fighting over a few valleys or plots of arable land. The new conflicts were merely the oldest conflicts in the world, those in which the stakes were access to basic resources for the survival of tribes and clans. But besides land and water, there are now other resources that are essential to the global economic system: petroleum, uranium, diamonds. Moreover, the tendency of local conflicts to become international once the purely internal phase is over is becoming a constant. Rwanda, Burundi, Congo, Angola, Uganda and Sudan have all had and are still having internal conflicts. Permeable borders and transnational interests engender an osmotic, synergistic movement that brings these conflicts together and reinforces them. The centre of Africa is on the brink of explosion and all efforts at mediation fail, one after the other. The intervention of Nelson Mandela, the SADC and OAU conferences, the special missions of European, American or UN envoys, all demonstrate the failure of international conflict resolution mechanisms. The American doctrine whereby 'only the Africans know what is good for Africa' is also revealing its limits – particularly as the Europeans themselves, witness Kosovo, do not know what is good for Europe. The tragic events that plunged the land of the fields of blackbirds (*Kosovo polje*) into mourning have been answered only by the pathetic posturing of a divided international community. In the midst of this exhibition of vehement gesticulation and avowed weakness, how can the humanitarian groups provide assistance to populations in distress and still be perceived as neutral and impartial (and not as suitable targets for snipers)?

New stakes are emerging that had been deliberately relegated to the background. An oil field here, a diamond deposit there, the potential route of an oil pipeline, an arsenal of nuclear warheads elsewhere. These are the real stakes in the new conflicts. More than ever, there is a desperate need to understand the dynamics of crises and the logic of the protagonists who provoke them or participate in them.

Continuum, contiguum, prevention: beware the buzz words

The dynamics of a renewed analysis of crises have led the Group to examine the relevance of the linear model of crisis interpretation that until recently has ruled the debates. In this much-vaunted continuum there are the periods before and during the crisis, the end of the crisis and, finally, the development phase. Although some cases follow this chronological linear pattern fairly closely, they are relatively rare. Analysis rapidly indicated numerous contexts where crisis zones and peaceful zones coexist and are often reversible. The concept of the 'contiguum' was born. The relevance of this concept was recognised at the June 1998 meeting of the United Nations Economic and Social Commission (ECOSOC).

How will these changes in the nature of the contexts of conflicts and the questioning of the relevance of established concepts influence our practices? How, for instance, can we shorten the food-aid phase by substituting as rapidly as possible strategies to strengthen coping mechanisms? How can the local dynamics of participant groups in national civil societies be taken into account, recognising both their strong points (knowledge of the environment) and their weaknesses (the risk of political partisanship)?

What is the best way to approach the complex and increasingly interwoven nature of the different types of disaster? Conflicts are often compounded by natural disasters, which themselves regularly occur in unstable agro-ecosystems and economies. An entire chapter of this book addresses the issue of prevention, the newly fashionable theme (pages 115–18). And not without reason. After all, the history of our own societies is a history of crises and conflicts. If the farmers of northeastern Brazil, after so many years of non-violent struggle to obtain land rights – rights for which dozens of them lost their lives to the Uzis and Kalashnikovs of the guards of the *latifundia* – decide that their only remaining option is to take up arms, should we go in advocating conflict prevention? We have also had to relativise the 'development–peace' relationship dear to the United Nations. Although, for example, promoting the management of rare resources and the protection of fragile ecosystems in development strategies will indubitably have a profound impact on the communities that inhabit the valley in question, this hardly means that it will lead to an environment conducive to peace. On the other hand, it will entail a cost to society, and no doubt also to the state, and thereby go against the prevailing rule of free circulation of capital and of comparative advantage that dominates the ultra-liberal approach.

Nevertheless, reflection on crisis prevention and, much more generally, on the nature of crises itself, must be based on a better understanding of the links (whether they exist or not, and whether they are direct or indirect) between crises arising from access to resources and crises in human societies. And the same understanding should govern strategies of intervention before the crisis, during the crisis – especially if it endures – and at the end of the conflict.

Professionalism, ethics and quality

How can we work in such contexts? On the basis of what ethical model, and according to what professional referents? Some humanitarian groups have a genuine mandate that confers on them a historical legitimacy. This is the good fortune of the ICRC, allowing it to develop a high standard of professionalism in many fields. It is also its weakness, if the perpetrators of violence flout its legitimacy and gun down ICRC delegates on the road or in a hospital to advance their political cause. Other humanitarian bodies have only a charter, a self-proclaimed code of solidarity with those in distress. This moral motivation has often led to noble actions. It has sometimes also served to disguise a serious lack of professionalism.

To tackle the problem, the ongoing development of new tools of analysis, programme development and evaluation is a fundamental task. The URD Group, through a system of exchange and concerted research, has undertaken this task. Moreover, by taking part in capacity building through a growing involvement in training activities, it is participating in the professionalisation of workers in the field. It is a matter of training teams in methods for analysing contexts, of strengthening analytic and conceptual capacities, of providing tools adaptable to various operations for the follow-up monitoring of interventions. It is also a matter of developing in-built monitoring parameters.

Challenging standardisation in a diverse and changing world

The URD Group views with great concern the attempt at universal standardisation that has been launched under the SPHERE project and the related attempt to establish a list of supposedly universal technical standards. The realities in the field are so diverse that in most instances an 'off-the-shelf' approach would provide no more than a partial solution to the problems. If agencies and donors start to respond to needs on the basis of a list of minimum standards, the likelihood that they will spend more time looking at these standards than at the reality of the situation is very high. Certainly, URD agrees that humanitarian actors should strive for quality; their credibility and accountability depend on it. But let us not be taken in by simplistic solutions, particularly the current fad of standards. Those proposed by the SPHERE project do not take into account the cultural diversity and changing nature of the crisis. They leave little room for proactive thinking in response to the prognosis of an existing situation. What is more, these standards apply only to particularly ideal (and therefore particularly rare) refugee camp conditions. Looking back on the past 20 years of humanitarian experience in four continents, the extraordinary diversity of situations is clear, as is the fact that most of them are excluded *de facto* from the area of application of the minimum standards of the SPHERE project. What could have been done in Afghanistan in the 1980s? What were the options during the exodus of the Krajina Serb population in 1995? How to work in Rwanda under fire in April 1994? What sort of activities should have been organised in situations such as the flight of the displaced people and Rwandan refugees in Zaïre at the end of 1996? Who could work in the Sierra Leonean bush today? Closer to us, what was the relevance of the SPHERE standards for 80 per cent of the Kosovan refugees, those hosted by Albanian families?

All strategies of standardisation lead to the risk of 'standardised thought'. The promoters of the SPHERE project have presented the setting of minimum standards as the ultimate tool to guarantee quality. We believe that quality depends on satisfying three conditions: better appraisal of the situations in their diversity and complexity (which requires further work in diagnosis methodologies); enhanced capacity for impact evaluation (which will require a small cultural revolution, fortunately already ongoing); and better human resources (with more training). This triple approach will result in greater professionalism, which depends on the mastery of know-how (within which standards assert their specific and important domain of validity) and a spectrum of other qualities: receptivity, analytic capacity, imagination, adaptability, vision, intuition, listening skills and a genuine ability to learn. What is definitely not recommended is adhesion to a preconceived menu of supposedly universal minimum standards. In the words of the philosopher, 'for every complex problem, there is a simple solution, and it is inevitably a bad one'. In a rapidly changing world, this has never been more true. Even more seriously, for the twenty or so member organisations of the URD Group, the fact that the SPHERE project has deliberately excluded from its 'sphere of interest' rehabilitation phases and survival activities is a cause for grave concern. This omission of the 'continuum–contiguum' issue is in flagrant contradiction of the entire body of research on humanitarian action in recent years.

Future challenges and tasks

The economic crisis that is affecting South-East Asia, Japan, Russia and soon, perhaps, South America has already called into question many of the dogmas of the economists and financial experts. The IMF itself was shaken. Today, its omniscience and omnipotence are at the centre of vigorous debate. Because of these ecological and economic crises, competition is reappearing for access to and possession of increasingly rare resources.

The centre of Africa is erupting while Eurasia west of the Urals sways uncertainly between between the crumbling Russian economy and a rising tide of fundamentalism from Afghanistan. This year alone, there has been a sharp increase in the number of international conflicts. These new wars are characterised by a high degree of unpredictability and a strong tendency to become regional crises. The current Great Lakes confrontation is a case in point and the Ethiopia/Eritrea conflict, with Sudan in the contagion zone, could be another.

The events of 1997 and 1998 pointed up the emergence of a new period of discontinuity: that which separates an era of crises that were essentially linked to internal conflicts (whatever their nature), from one of large-scale natural disasters, major economic and social disasters, and the risk of regional flare-ups. The floods in China and Bangladesh, the increasingly serious consequences of El Niño on fragile ecosystems in South America (underlined by Hurricane MITCH) and the vast forest fires in Indonesia offer a demonstration, if one were needed, of the fragility of man's domain. The scale of these disasters compels our humility. How can Western humanitarian aid face up to situations that affect dozens of millions of victims? Advances in our understanding of the greenhouse effect and climate changes do not encourage optimism.

For its part, the era of technological disasters, of which the explosion at Bophal and the Chernobyl meltdown were a foretaste, is still to come. The challenges are many and the need for timely preventive measures is pressing. It is in this direction and with this open-mindedness that the ERD Group began its work at the end of 1993. This is the dynamism it wishes to share through this book. And it is in this direction that it intends to continue to work in the future.

The book itself does not end with a definitive conclusion but, on the contrary, leads to new themes to be explored and further research to be pursued. The issue of partnership in contexts of unrest, and of its limits even in development situations, has been analysed at length in *The Dilemmas of Humanitarian Aid*. The entire Group will continue to explore this key issue in the future. The importance of maintaining unceasing discussion on matters of ethics has been firmly underscored, particularly on the occasion of fruitful debates on neutrality and impartiality. As for the relationship between private humanitarian action (undertaken by associations or organisations such as the ICRC) and state humanitarian action (in particular the role of the military during as well as at the end of crises), this topic will be the focus of future studies.

PART I

Towards a New Analysis of Crisis

Edited by

BERNARD HUSSON AND CLAIRE PIROTTE

The way in which NGOs interpreted crises in the past no longer corresponds to the reality in the field. It is obvious that we need to revise our methods of analysis, our reflexes and our ready-made solutions if we wish to mitigate the impact of crises or resolve them. A different interpretation of crises – rethinking the way in which they are perceived by the actors, the donors and the media – is both necessary, because of the increasingly confusing nature of current events, and urgent, to avoid repeating patterns of action that yield mixed results. Among NGOs, those dealing in emergencies are of course the most concerned by the changing nature of crises and the method of intervention when a conflict breaks out. They cannot afford to omit in-depth analysis without incurring the risk of acting rashly or being exploited by special-interest groups. What is 'humanitarian assistance' if the aid it brings is a bargaining chip for the parties in conflict, or if convoys must move under military protection?

But it is not only the work of these humanitarian agencies that is being called into question. That of development organisations is also being challenged, just as forcefully. Conflicts break out in countries where long-term actions have been nurtured carefully and where positive results seemed guaranteed. Confronted with the violence of conflicts they thought belonged to the past, organisations can no longer be unaware that their actions may cause tensions, and that conflicting interests among the populations with which they work may still be rife, in spite of an appearance of harmony.

The Great Lakes crisis was a milestone for all the humanitarian agencies and development organisations. On this occasion, NGOs of all stripes came together to deliberate on history, sociology and geo-

9

political analysis, and to engage in pragmatic discussion based on their varied experiences. An explosive, sometimes provocative mix, they examined their position, the result of the twofold legacy they themselves had helped to promote and which was now being challenged. The first component of this legacy is based on the long-held tenet that 'development is peace and peace is development.' The second stems from the French 'civil defence' system which, via the 'French Doctors' and SAMU (Secours et assistance médicale d'urgence, the French emergency medical service), promotes the worthy conviction prevalent in medical circles that by combining speed and efficiency one can save the life of every human being in distress.

The succession of opinions presented in this book is not intended to display a common stand but is an attempt to decipher ther very notion of crisis (B. Husson, A. Marty, C. Pirotte and F. Grunewald) as it has come to be understood since 1945 (J.-Ch. Ruffin). Crisis cannot be dissociated from dvelopment (C. Fusillier and M. Duffield) but, whatever the situations they face, affected populations as always try to preserve a certain degree of harmony (P. Vincent), even when the conflict brings economic activity to a virtual halt (F. Grunewald).

When a crisis breaks out, NGOs can disregard neither the history of the affected populations (J. B. Richardier), nor the strategies of the parties to the conflict, nor those of the states (P. Laurent). How, then, in an extremely complex situation, can NGOs avoid losing sight of their intentions (P. Biberson)?

Beyond differences of appreciation, all these observations have one point in common. Crisis must no longer be viewed only as a period of destruction, but also as an occasion when initiatives emerge which we must learn to detect. This joint approach leads us to suggest, further on in this book, new objectives and modalities for intervention during and after crises.

◆◆◆

1 • Observations on Crises

BERNARD HUSSON, ANDRÉ MARTY AND CLAIRE PIROTTE

There are two common types of crisis: some are predominantly *economic*, due to a number of factors such as weather-related devastation, that may or may not be predictable; others are predominantly *structural* – as when demographic growth exceeds production capacity without the possibility of emigration, or political destructuring occurs, with conflicts that may or may not be negotiable. All crises, however, share certain characteristics:

- a crisis is temporary;
- it is unstable;
- it can rarely be resolved without the help of an intermediary;
- although everyone has an opinion, its outcome is uncertain;
- its resolution will mark a change, in that the outcome cannot be simply a return to the pre-existing situation.

These characteristics represent traumatic events for the societies which experience them. They give rise to hitherto unknown chain reactions of violence which have nothing to do with ordinary modes of functioning. It is therefore out of the question to trivialise the event, in view of its exceptional and original nature. Hannah Arendt wrote that the real significance of an event always exceeds all the past causes one can assign to it.

Open crisis – murderous conflict or civil war – is an exceptional occurrence in the life of a society, even if the violence goes on for months, indeed years. It marks a break in the ordinary organisation and *modus operandi* of this society. It gives rise to new authorities and new organisations, including military ones. It underscores the emergence of new relations between components of society which disagree, seemingly implacably, on how to build the future. In this respect, the first reaction of the observers, whether institutional or independent, is that 'the future will not resemble the past'. In their analysis it is as though the outbreak of the crisis profoundly modified the entire equation and ultimately cancelled out the past.

However, the period during which a crisis intensifies must be considered in its long-term context. Every crisis has a history. It brings to light existing contradictions, latent rifts. The real causes of crises are indeed often different from their apparent causes. What then, one must ask oneself, really changes? Crisis, according to E. Morin, is a critical moment of ambiguity and uncertainty. It reveals and sheds light on the contradictions of the moment and on latent rifts. It can also be caused by the wish to reproduce society as it is, the confusion helping to create a new order that closely resembles the old. Crisis, as the 'moment of truth', can bring about a new order just as it can recreate the past. It can be an instrument for maintaining established order, just as it can be an instrument for change.

For example, in the absence of government, outlying regions of Somalia are witnessing the comeback of traditional chieftains. Peru is experiencing a return to an authoritarian regime rather than the expansion of democracy. We must therefore avoid limiting our vision to the present moment, even if it is the reason for the intervention. The crisis should not be divorced from its historical and socio-political context. Interaction is necessary between the factual and the structural, between actors and systems, between the short- and the long-term, and between the local and the global levels.

A crisis is always serious

The outbreak of a crisis is always serious. It means that a society's ability to resolve its tensions is exceeded, making the management of daily life difficult for individuals and groups. The rules which govern collective life no longer function; fear and hostility are intensified; the living conditions of the most vulnerable or exposed groups deteriorate; their very lives may be in danger.

The outbreak of a crisis indicates that the functioning or the evolution of society have become intolerable for some. During the last fifty years a legitimate fear of war has led to a denial of tensions or, when they have erupted into crises, to attempts to solve them by mobilising armed intervention forces to stem the escalation of violence and organise support in the form of emergency aid. The hope for a world without war has overshadowed the fact that societies change, depending on the moment and their socio-economic circumstances, through negotiation between social groups or under the pressure of open crisis. By taking into consideration only the first scenario, we deny ourselves the option of managing the crises that break out.

Crisis as a factor of change

Development begets change, a source of tension. Crises are often perceived as negative, yet they are unavoidable and occasionally bene-ficial. Development has been one of the 'weapons' for containing crises. Like any evolutionary process, development inevitably leads to rifts. Developers have been inclined to ignore this consequence of their actions, focusing only on adapting their interventions to the needs of the populations with which they work. By dint of associating the words peace and development, conflicts have come to be interpreted as failures when they should be integrated as a potential strategic element to be utilised by the actors. Perhaps we should stop thinking of armed conflict as an aberration, even if peace is naturally desirable and the peaceful resolution of conflict is a sign of a society's maturity.

Crisis breeds defence capabilities and leads to innovation

We observe that local survival, resistance, organisation, support and negotiation capabilities continue to function during periods of tension and conflict, just as they do in times of stability. These capabilities are not static – societies tap unsuspected resources to survive. Conflict sit-uations are sometimes even more favourable to the expression of such capabilities because survival situations require innovation. From this point of view, what is lacking today is a working method that allows us to put to use in peacetime the experience gained in conflict. In particu-lar, the status that women acquire in situations of conflict is lost in the ensuing period of peace.

The received wisdom which opposes crisis and development leads to two questions:

- Is it really certain that development projects can only be envisaged in times of economic and political stability?

- Is it wise to neglect local capacities for innovation when they are being demonstrated – sometimes in times of conflict, which also happens to be when they most need strengthening?

◆◆◆

2 ◆ Development Is Not Peace
FRANÇOIS GRUNEWALD

This debate was settled by the distressing events in Rwanda. This small country, one of the most assisted countries in Africa, has received economic aid with a positive impact that has been widely stressed. Extensive reinforcement of the social fabric had been undertaken in such key areas as the creation and expansion of people's decentralised savings and loan banks, support for the structuring of cottage industries, and more generally the elaboration of local development plans.

It is possible to improve people's living conditions, possible sometimes to reduce inequality, to acknowledge the capacity for initiative of the very poor, without for all that bridging other gaps. Concentrating efforts on the economic and social sectors masked other factors of crisis that erupted under the pressure of malevolent propaganda. All the 'positive' activities were carried out 'as if all was well'; the reinforcement of social cohesion was not taken into account.

Development dynamics do not necessarily produce peace. For that, three objectives must be met. The first is the basis for the discourse and actions of the development organisations; the second and third often elicit lip service but rarely result in action:

◆ development must be economically viable, ecologically reproducible and socially just;

◆ development must promote civil rights and the freedom of expression of the citizens;

◆ development must promote the dissemination of a philosophy of peace.

Any development strategy that does not meet these objectives does not participate in crisis prevention and may result in the need for actions to respond to an emergency situation.

3 • The Pattern of Conflicts since 1945

JEAN-CHRISTOPHE RUFFIN

It is often said that the number of conflicts has been increasing, particularly since the end of the Cold War. This assessment must be taken with caution. Since 1945 there have been other periods of conflict as serious as that which we have been experiencing in the past five years. From this perspective, it would be more appropriate to speak of Cold Wars in the plural. Indeed, since 1945 the international scene has gone through a series of alternating stable and unstable phases.

Basically, there have been three major conflict phases since 1945. Each lasted about fifteen years and was marked by an initial phase of increased instability followed by a phase of relative stability.

◆ *1945 to 1950* was a period of instability. The year 1945 marked the end of the 'order' opposing the Allies and the Axis powers they eventually defeated. Two events marked the beginning of East–West bipolarity: the formation of the Sino-Soviet bloc in 1949, followed by the beginning of the Korean War in 1950. Between these two dates, we shifted from one international order to another, and conflicts multiplied (on the European continent, along the arc of containment, in the decolonisation zones).

◆ *1950 to 1960* was a period of relative stability. There were peripheral conflicts and conflicts resulting from decolonisation, but they were of little consequence to East–West relations.

◆ *1960 to 1965* was a period of instability. Sino-Soviet relations broke down in 1960. The Third World was the scene of formidable competition not only between East and West, but among the leaders of the Communist world as well. Conflicts and armed movements flourished, particularly in Africa (as in the decolonisation of the Belgian Congo) but also with the Cuban revolution in 1959, and the resumption of war in Vietnam. From 1965, however, there was a resurgence of American domination: the United States intervened in Santo Domingo and in several coups in Latin America.

◆ *1965 to 1975* was a period of relative stability. One conflict endured and dominated the international scene: the Vietnam war.

♦ *1975 to 1980* was a period of instability. Most of the conflicts on the international scene today first broke out during this period. In 1975 the Watergate scandal was followed by the pull-out of American troops from Vietnam; it signalled a major decline in the power of the West. This period was further marked by a series of revolutions: the Ethiopian revolution in 1974 and the shift of alliances in the region; the decolonisation of the Spanish Sahara in 1975; conflicts in southern Africa following the Portuguese revolution; the fall of Somoza in Nicaragua; the invasion of Afghanistan by Soviet troops in 1979 following the Iranian revolution; the invasion of Cambodia by the Vietnamese; conflicts in Sri Lanka and other countries. In 1980, the United States under President Reagan took a harder line towards the Communist bloc and a new balance of power emerged.

♦ *1980 to 1990* was a period of relative stability at the cost of low-intensity conflicts. The period ended with the collapse of the Communist bloc.

This brief summary of recent history shows that, on the international scene, phases of stability and instability have followed one another in a fairly regular pattern. These phases were not imposed by the Cold War alone. During this period, conflict prevention stemmed, in a way, from the conflicts themselves. Between 1950 and 1960, the containment policy guaranteed international order; during the period from 1965 to 1975, the Vietnam war prevented conflict by providing a focal point for world-wide hostility and even allowed for some degree of understanding between the two superpowers, which negotiated the Helsinki agreements; during the period from 1980 to 1990, low-intensity conflicts played the same preventive role, inasmuch as they limited hostilities to a certain degree.

Since 1990, this pattern is no longer valid: this is the first characteristic of the new type of conflict. The occurrence of conflicts is accelerating; the world, the Third World in particular, appears highly volatile – as though any disagreement, any problem with neighbours or minorities, might lead automatically to a conflict. Previously, in order to produce a conflict, these sources of local tension had to exist, of course, but they were overridden by the international context. Henceforth, any attempt to make an inventory of conflicts is bedevilled by their dizzying numbers. The difficulty of the task is evidenced by the size and volume of the *Mondes rebelles* catalogue. In this climate of unbridled hostility, the absence of major players is noteworthy: no outside influence is able any longer to organise or moderate it. Conflicts appear to have become autonomous.

The second characteristic of this new type of conflict is the possibility of 'extreme' – total and widespread – war. In the 1980s in particular, conflicts remained localised; they could not acquire any real scope, either regionally or in terms of armaments. Conflicts were confined to so-called 'low-intensity' levels. Arms were usually light personal weapons, except in the case of the Afghan Mujaheddin who used Stinger missiles in the mid-1980s. Wars were conducted without navy or airforce, and the capacity for destruction of conflicts was rather low. The consequences for the civilian population were of course no less serious. Today, there is no longer any control over the means at the disposal of the combatants, which leads to a higher risk of conflicts spreading. Fighters can obtain all the weapons they want. Whereas in the 1980s they were often funded by outside allies, they now organise their own business dealings. There is therefore a strong possibility that the intensity of contemporary conflicts will increase.

This is all the more pronounced as the interests in these conflicts are not local and planetary, as they were during the Cold War, but local and regional. Regional powers frequently interfere in these conflicts; they are often the only ones to intervene in earnest, with the ambition of regional domination. In Liberia, for example, in the guise of a peace-keeping power, Nigeria is intervening with the aim of reasserting its regional hegemony. In the same fashion, Pakistan continues to play an important role in the Afghan conflict although the internal struggles in that country are beyond the control of the international community. In regions where armaments are sophisticated, local confrontations can lead to regional build-ups, which can sometimes involve nuclear arsenals, as between India and Pakistan. The potential for a flare-up is much greater than it was during the Cold War, when the balance of superpowers was a stabilising factor.

Faced with the expansion of this new type of conflict, must one intervene? Is there a way to prevent the escalation – and, if so, how?

◆◆◆

4 • Development in the Face of Crisis
CHRISTIAN FUSILLIER

Actions which foster development are rarely linked explicitly with one or more development strategies requiring the government of the country to have a broadly outlined policy; to state specific goals for rural and urban development; and to define the coordination of various sectors.

In the absence of a general framework, interventions – often initiated from the outside – are based on isolated diagnoses and one observes the proliferation of as many strategies as there are donors, consultants or NGOs, each with its own logic. The governments of developing countries often merely administer the budgets which they receive in the form of loans or subsidies rather than taking aboard the ideas or strategies introduced by the intervention itself. Without minimal coordination, a patchwork of all kinds of projects can be a powerful fermenting agent for future crises.

The contradictions and negative side-effects brought about by development are not only due to bad coordination among the participants. It is not unusual, within the same programme, to observe practices which tend to reinforce social disparities or create new ones. For example, in order to optimise the impact of a given project, a certain number of village communities might be chosen. The resulting achievements will artificially differentiate those villages from their neighbours, frequently leading to disagreement, particularly concerning land ownership and economic infrastructures. Another adverse effect of development interventions that might result in future crisis arises from time management. Agencies carry out quick interventions with big financial and human resources, then disengage and entrust the local population with the task of pursuing the action. If no provision is made beforehand to ensure financial and organisational continuity, conflicts and embryonic crises will result. It is important to respect the rhythm of change, and even to abstain from intervening altogether if sufficient pre-conditions for success are not met.

Development activities, even when they are coordinated, are no guarantee against crisis, although they may be based on a local desire for change. Any development process necessarily leads to phases of instability, adjustment and reorganisation. The crises which developers face are long-term and predictable; they result from:

- *major weather hazards* of a magnitude which cannot be predicted, although their effects can be tempered by prevention strategies such as early warning systems, emergency food reserves, debt rescheduling, loan guarantees or animal vaccination campaigns;

- *economic problems* – monetary devaluation, loss of markets or competitiveness – which may or may not be well managed;

- *periods of evolutionary change*, decisive moments in time when profound imbalances emerge (between population growth and natural resources, for example).

Although often aware of the problems, the inhabitants, absorbed by more pressing short-term priorities such as food security, only take them into account when it is already too late.

Social crisis, a symptom of change – good or bad – breaks out when a situation presents one of the three following characteristics: unfair distribution of resources; uncompromising denial of political expression; or brutal deprivation of social recognition. The activity of the developers should therefore be integrated into programmes which contribute to a better sharing of resources by making them accessible to minorities. Developers rarely comprehend that armed conflict can occur and that a crisis can be used for a reorganisation which would not have been possible before the crisis broke out. Whether before, during or after a crisis, it is essential to take into account the strategies and interests of all the actors concerned before launching an action, and not to overestimate the impact of that action on the population: often selective, it will be marginal compared with the social and political interests at stake.

◆◆◆

5 ◆ The Crisis of International Aid
MARK DUFFIELD[1]

Emergency situations defy conventional development theory, which posits a normative process of evolution based on the hypothesis of the universality of social progress, leading from poverty and vulnerability to security and well-being. The mechanisms of international aid, constructed in accordance with this idea of development, have been powerless to deal with the rising tide of crises. Developmental change often provokes crisis at the heart of political, social and economic structures. Prolonged tensions brought about by social-economic inequality and predatory practices impel local populations to resist changes over which they have no control. In situations such as these, which destroy social networks and systems, humanitarian aid can be a target for violence or for appropriation by actors in the crisis which the aid is supposed to counteract.

There are two reasons for this. First, limiting emergency aid to the distribution of survival goods and services is the result of reasoning inherited from natural disaster relief, which attaches little or no importance to political and social factors. The interventions in Angola and Somalia are proof of this. Second, emergency aid is a concept generated by development ideology itself. In their approach to societies, development agencies have actually proved themselves incapable of understanding political crises or even civil wars as other than passing anomalies to which one can only apply programmes designed for natural disasters. Thus, in defending the concept of the emergency-to-development continuum, the United Nations Development Programme (UNDP) has interpreted emergency situations as temporary interruptions of the development process. Such an interpretation can cause long-term dependence and weaken the capacity of the local population to adapt. Its cause is not an attempt to understand crises in order to contribute to their resolution, but the defensive reaction of an institution jeopardised by the transfer of resources from development to emergency organisations.

Towards the end of the 1980s the first cross-border operations commissioned by the United Nations in South Sudan, Ethiopia and Angola, sometimes called 'corridors of peace', represented an historical turning point. The UN aligned itself with the independent NGOs and recognised the need to intervene in unresolved conflicts. But such intervention is based on the negotiated right to intervene, which presupposes that the parties at war accept neutral humanitarian intervention. Enormous difficulties were encountered and the programmes were provided with military protection from the beginning of the 1990s.

This transformation of the agencies resulted in the normalisation of violence: today, there are about fifty conflicts which are considered as normal. Consequently, in order to draw international attention, a local crisis has to reach record-breaking levels of barbarity. As the sole response to conflicts, the negotiated right to intervene is becoming more and more sophisticated, with an unprecedented integration of supposedly neutral humanitarian aid in the dynamics of violence. Thus, one sees former military personnel serving as security advisers and adjustable aid programmes which can be activated or withdrawn depending on the intensity of the fighting. For local actors, therefore, controlling and manipulating aid has become crucial to the economy of the conflict. This operational and political flexibility has eroded the idea of collective international responsibility, as shown by events in Bosnia.

The UN Charter and the Geneva Conventions have given way to intervention criteria based on media exposure and internal political interests. And although they will not admit it, the financial and media dependence of NGOs, and their ability to work in very diverse situations, have enabled governments to use humanitarian aid programmes to serve their national interests.

Considering conflicts simply as irrational events and waiting them out hampers the research and practical action which should be undertaken immediately. A sense of collective international responsibility must be restored regarding poverty and violence. We must come up with a new code of ethics to deal with the complex reality of civil wars and prolonged political crises. For this, solidarity is certainly a better guide than neutrality.

◆◆◆

6 ◆ Who Determines the Objectives?
Pascal Vincent

As long as the logic of aid, euphemistically termed 'support', is based on the values of Northern developers, the populations of the South and the East will be compelled to misappropriate it to their own ends.

From beneficiary to partner

Adapting what was once a totally ethnocentrist managerial approach, the North has gradually reached a compromise, recognising the right of the beneficiaries to define their needs and their development through participation and integrated action. The objectives of present practices tend to give the beneficiaries responsibility through a partnership which advocates equality through dialogue and consultation.

In the field, this discourse has been expressed in the form of words, deeds and behaviour. It has been heard, seen and interpreted, often endured, occasionally shared, but in any case taken up and integrated by the beneficiaries. For at the same time as the North is experimenting with a discourse and an approach regarding development, local strategies are being formulated to enable a better day-to-day command of new parameters, to control potentialities and get around difficulties. Thus, the discourse of the developers is matched by that of the local actors and of the target groups.

The official line of assistance programmes is being progressively assimilated by the affected communities. They perceive, adopt, interpret the guiding principles of the approach through slogans. 'Rise – we will help you', for instance, defines the participatory attitude sought by those in charge of a project, and which is materialised by the personal contribution of the population concerned, prior to action itself. More generally, a project with a managerial approach is likened to 'a stranger who offers an elderly man a cane to help him get up', a participatory village project to 'a stranger who does not proffer a cane, but throws it away and tells the old man to make an effort to go and get it'.

(Mis)using development?

The discourse of local leaders identified as interlocutors by external operators is subsequently often used by their constituency to take advantage of the proposed plan of action. A nomadic population, for instance, targeted for a project to support settlement, requested a loan to help them in their agricultural activities (in keeping with the purported objectives of the project). But their real aim was to rebuild the herds they had lost to drought; for them, the loss of their livestock was the major obstacle to a return to nomadic life. They therefore sought to use the project to achieve their own ends and not those of the project. Another case is that of a village in Mali which, during the process of decentralisation, tried to use a health project to obtain a health centre, in order to position itself as a potential district centre.

Furthermore, to reinforce their strategies, populations seek to ally themselves with national actors whom they use as intermediaries, considering them as 'lackeys of the Whites' (the expatriates). They develop strategies to take advantage of their position and profit both financially and socially.

◆◆◆

22

7 • A Better Understanding of the Economic Impact of War

François Grunewald

Increasingly, 'non-growth' and 'conflict for resources' will go hand in hand. The economic deterioration which accompanies conflicts leads, in these contexts, to growing food insecurity. Moreover, war now threatens the means of subsistence. Until recently, acts of destruction were mainly aimed at weakening the enemy. By inflicting suffering on civilian populations, one could hope to induce the enemy to give up, to negotiate, or even to surrender. Although this mode of conducting hostilities still exists, another has emerged, in which the aim of the conflict is the destruction, and if possible the pure and simple annihilation of the opponent. Means of production, water systems, herds or health infrastructures all become targets, all the more so as by destroying them one kills, starves or obliges the *others* – the unwanted, those who are different – to flee. Furthermore, artificially induced famine which attracts aid to help fuel the conflict is a frequent scenario. In this context, actions aimed not only at supporting immediate survival but also at preserving life in the future are particularly complex, as wars aim precisely at preventing both.

All these conflicts have a common characteristic: the majority are becoming poorer while a few grow rich. Although in most cases this rift occurs along the general fracture lines of social differences which existed prior to the crisis, the appearance of new actors born of the conflict, particularly armed forces or gangs, can bring about a redistribution of wealth.

The organisation of economic activities is then divided into three strata which may influence each other:

- a survival economy for the populations;
- an economy designed to fuel the war machine;
- a speculative economy in private hands (militias that may or may not be related to organised crime).

International aid, including that portion which is misappropriated to finance the conflict itself, plays an important role on these three levels. But the volume of this aid should not mask other phenomena, such as the hijacking of aid as much by the populations themselves as by the aid agencies.

Informal economies are created

During a conflict, available goods and services become scarce. Such a situation offers opportunities for gain to those who work outside the law. Production processes generally being seriously slowed down, the only sector that functions is that of supplies – frequently illegal – and speculation. Difficult times often also reveal the immense capacity for adaptation and the ingenuity of a population Consequently, from Yugoslavia to Afghanistan, from Angola to Somalia, new forms of informal economies and numerous new sectors of activity emerged to compensate, at least in part, for the effects of war on the availability of supplies.

When farmers are afraid to stock their produce, they cultivate tubers, which can be left in the fields until they are consumed. If militias and soldiers raid the tuber crops, the farmers plant a mix of sweet cassava which is immediately edible, and bitter cassava which is toxic unless properly prepared. Soldiers do not have the time to prepare the bitter cassava which must undergo a long process of drying, cooking and re-drying – the only way to eliminate the cyanide it contains. Agricultural rehabilitation operations must take into account such mechanisms to prevent the hijacking of aid. Although armed groups attack food convoys or warehouses in order to feed their troops and sell the food to buy weapons, they rarely attack trucks carrying agricultural tools or stocks of seed, which are much more difficult to sell.

Understanding the nature of the opposing forces

Wars that drag on generate situations that frequently lead to the collapse of the traditional concept of nation-state. This collapse produces two types of scenario:

◆ the proliferation of mini-fiefdoms, each of which seeks all the attributes – administrative, military and police – of a sovereign state;

◆ the complete disappearance of the state and of order, which complicates the identification of responsible interlocutors with well-defined political lines.

Outside observers refer to this as a 'destructured' conflict. In fact, these conflicts are very structured. The organised structures that usually serve as references are simply replaced by others based on ethnicity, lineage, street, neighbourhood, village of origin, gang and so on. The production and redistribution of wealth and spoils is the work of these structures.

The immediate post-war period is not one of peace

In devastated countries, for exhausted populations, the end of hostilities does not necessarily mean a return to normal life. It is easier to win a war than to achieve peace. Indeed, conflict resolution requires coping with extremely complex problems: access for all to the economic and agricultural resources of a whole country; shared access to bilateral and multilateral aid, particularly for reconstruction; the enforcement of peace agreements that frequently involve the incorporation of former combatants into the national army; the integration of others into the work force through special training and the provision of equipment; and assistance to returning refugees. Experience shows how difficult this is. Broken promises lead to resentment and acrimony, all the more dangerous because in such times weapons are readily available – the case of Mali is a good example. Even more serious, entire areas are rendered sterile and unfit for farming because of mines and unexploded ordinance. Thousands of rural families will continue, long after the war is over, to pay a heavy price.

The physical and psychological effects of prolonged conflicts on populations, and the deterioration of infrastructures and production systems, have devastating consequences that must be taken into account. Agricultural support systems – popular education in farming methods, loans, buying and selling of seed, vaccination of livestock – no longer function. Markets no longer receive supplies, or else are controlled by organised crime. The buying power of potential buyers is very low.

Colossal means are needed to rebuild such economies. Since the Marshall Plan for Europe and the reconstruction programme in Japan, no programme has been financed on such a large scale. Although considerable, typical reconstruction plans – such as those for Cambodia, undertaken following the 1991 peace accord and the 1993 elections, or for former Yugoslavia – fall short of the needs and the promises made, leading to a build-up of delays and resentments that jeopardise the chances of long-lasting peace.

◆◆◆

8 ✦ Humanitarian Aid Cannot Be Reduced to 'Trucking'

Jean-Baptiste Richardier

Emergency aid always has a social context. The survival strategies of populations, especially rural ones, are invaluable advantages which must be sustained. How to make use of the positive energy generated by the perspective of reconstruction, people's capacity to adapt, and the human dignity often revealed by disaster?

Extreme emergency being much less common than situations of enduring distress, one must be careful not to rush into action without careful consideration. In the past few years the logistics of solidarity actions have gone off course, and their significance has been clouded, mainly because of misunderstandings on the part of agencies, donors and public authorities – but also on the part of the media and, finally, public opinion. The dependence of the population, the worsening of destabilisation and the rise of corruption define the limits and the side-effects of massive emergency aid actions. But there is also a danger that the meaning of the action might be distorted, no matter how necessary we think it is.

The first risk factor is a commitment that lies somewhere between 'Manichean empathy' and 'sanitary colonialism', leading us to believe that we can control good and bad, the support of a supposedly just cause overriding our competence and our respect for the limits of our mandate.

The second risk is that of aggravating the breakdown of social dialogue. Aid operations anticipate the needs of the beneficiaries and can contribute to weakening the fragile relations between citizens and a state that is doubly discredited: first it is proved that it can no longer fulfil its role; second, it is seen to resort to actions decided by foreigners. The risk may be acceptable in situations of extreme crisis, but the operators must immediately make every effort to preserve the fabric of local structures.

Third, there is a big risk that aid operations conceal suffering and misery behind a discreet veil of charity. Without giving way to tropical romanticism, one observes that, most often, poor societies are not discriminatory, thanks to the strong social ties they maintain in the face of adversity. In our societies, the rise of exclusion and individualism, and the deterioration of the social contract, lead us to develop humanitarian aid as a way of keeping our distance. The media-humanitarian aid duo leads us to reduce the meaning of our actions to first-aid operations and to glorify our air bridges as all-powerful. The victims are only of interest to us because of the help we can give them, not because of their history or their future, and even less because of any sense of solidarity we may feel towards them.

Therefore, there is a great risk of creating a reassuring vision of a world in which the 'humanitarian' reigns triumphant – doing the minimum, sometimes without rhyme or reason, and gaining wide media coverage with a stop-gap 'better than nothing' attitude. By encouraging fatalism and indifference, the humanitarian adventure show overshadows what real images of the world could teach us. Even more serious are the recent deviations where so-called 'humanitarian' action has merged with political action or implicitly substituted for it, while the lack of political action was cloaked in humanitarian virtues.

By steadfastly pursuing an alliance between those who are helped and those who try to help them – an attitude that preserves their respective abilities to think, to experience and to exist – humanitarian action can earn the right to be considered as a genuine act of solidarity.

◆◆◆

9 ◆ The Humanitarian Impasse
Pierre Laurent

Humanitarian assistance has reached an impasse – not a momentary impasse, but a structural one that could jeopardise its existence in the long term. Zaïre is a blatant example of this, after a series of more or less injudicious actions in former Yugoslavia, Rwanda and Chechnya. Multilateral, bilateral or non-governmental action had the common goal – which was more or less explicit, more or less codified in international law – of assisting populations that were the victims of natural or man-made disasters, no matter what the circumstances. Today, this mission is hampered because the humanitarians no longer have access to the victims. The theatres of intervention are resounding proof of this. The reasons are numerous.

The first element of explanation is that humanitarian organisations have become – in the eyes of states, beneficiaries, rebellions and guerrilla movements – a component of the elusive 'international community'. Elusive because this much-used – and misused – term merely symbolises a virtual power that would rule the planet, a journalistic simplification which conceals the real responsibilities. The field of international relations, including the poorest countries, is only made up of a roster of states. The United Nations and other regional organisations are, for all practical purposes, only a sum of national interests.

When states have no special interests in countries in crisis where humanitarians are intervening, the absence of a common policy among them is obvious. Therefore, humanitarian organisations are increasingly becoming instruments of the parties to the conflicts and, with time, the channels through which these parties can influence international decisions, or even national resolutions.

The exploitation of humanitarian agencies differs according to the objectives. They are pampered, helped and given full cooperation when it is necessary to create a good image, particularly *vis-à-vis* international institutions. They are taken hostage when negotiations are at hand. And, occasionally, their expatriate staff are murdered when embarrassing witnesses must be eliminated. In recent years these scenarios have been taken to new heights world-wide. The humanitarians, especially the galaxy of non-governmental organisations, have obviously helped to set themselves up as a potential prey. Their allure in the eyes of public opinion and the media has led to their growing influence. Unwittingly, they have been cast in this role through the negligence of politicians. When elected officials have opted for a *laissez-faire* policy, confusion, power struggles and economic interests, the citizens have come up with a strategy of solidarity, international vision and a need for transparency.

Through this change in their position, humanitarian organisations have become true representatives of the voiceless. But they have also invited cynical manipulation by guerrilla or opposition movements, and by states, which have taken these volunteer spokespeople hostage all the more easily as they are usually the last foreign representatives to stay on in crisis situations.

The assimilation of humanitarian organisations with the international community has been further emphasised by the confusion of humanitarian assistance with intervention in the name of humanity. 'Humanitarian assistance' is a 'humble, unflagging action guided by the conviction that it is appropriate to prevent the excessive flouting of the most fundamental rights. Its means, dispensed with a concern for impartiality, are medical care, medicines, food, shelter, etc.'[2] 'Intervention in the name of humanity' can be defined as an act of rightful defence, of peacekeeping, of restoration of law, of peaceful change. It often calls for coercive military means under the responsibility of the United Nations (Chapters VI and VII of the UN Charter). The confusion between these two forms of action has greatly tarnished the image of the ICRC and of the non-governmental organisations.

UN agencies, by their very nature, cannot have the same impartiality and humanitarian spirit. This is why the humanitarian bodies consider it wrong that they should have to use coercive measures such as protected humanitarian corridors or convoys under military escort in order to reach the victims. It is a matter of their identity *vis-à-vis* the victims or the warring parties, a question of conscience and ethics. Such measures can indeed be effective in the short term, in a given place. But, in the long term, confusion between the military and the humanitarian actors deprives the latter of access by peaceful means in other areas.

But the stakes are even more complex. There cannot be two approaches, one for the UN agencies and another for the NGOs. Experience shows that the image of the 'humanitarian community' is one and the same among the victims and the warring parties, and that there is no room for variations and subtleties. This being the case, how to reach the victims without jeopardising the fundamental principles of humanitarian assistance once these organisations have become vulnerable, once their integrity can no longer protect them and once military operations tend to blur their identity? Some seek an answer in a law that would protect them, an irony considering that many NGOs have fought against just such a solution. Confronted by the panic ensuing from the present gridlock, we are witnessing a proliferation of proposals for security regulations to protect expatriate and local personnel. Although such instruments are probably necessary to limit risk, they in no way guarantee access to – and the protection of – the victims of conflict. Would more visible markings on our vehicles, for instance, or protective enclosures around our houses, deter military, paramilitary or political forces? Although such a law is not the sole solution, a durable solution does depend on it.

◆◆◆

10 • Keeping Sight of Our Intentions
PHILIPPE BIBERSON INTERVIEWED BY CLAIRE PIROTTE

The intentions that motivate us

The ideology that motivates the actors in an emergency can be sum-marised as 'the need to provide a solution here and now to safeguard the vital needs of individuals without necessarily considering what will happen afterwards'. It is founded on a vision of the individual as being representative of the entire human race. In this respect, each individual deserves help to protect his life. To save an individual is to save the portion of humanity he represents. What he will become later, good or evil, is not envisaged.

The ideology of development on the other hand implies a purpose, a meaning, a direction for the whole of humanity: one must 'help to' – help to achieve more freedom, peace, social justice, and so on. But one observes that until now the emphasis has been placed mainly on the socio-economic criteria of development, a weak level of these criteria being indicative of 'underdevelopment'.

Underlying both these visions is the same intention, one that moti-vates all the actors to help others to achieve more freedom, to reject fatalism, to refuse oppression or segregation, to support individuals and populations who seek emancipation. This intention is of a universal and noble character; it is political with a progressive stance; and is expressed through diverse actions and skills.

The betrayal of objectives

Although a universal intention exists, it is sometimes betrayed by its implementation. Favouring the means can result in a biased response to requests. One's intentions should be carefully analysed to avoid pitfalls, such as placing populations in a situation of need. Liberia is a case in point, where we know that combatants deliberately starved popula-tions to attract and plunder foreign aid. The primary intent, which is to save people from starvation, is laudable. But should one respond blindly, without posing the problem in terms of ethics, denying freedom and freedom of expression the importance accorded to the ful-filment of vital needs? Responding to this type of demand without analysing the heterogeneity of the situation places the beneficiaries in a position of dependence on basic necessities.

30

Another form of betrayal of objectives can arise from the use by certain states of the 'compassion factor' which is the basis for emergency and development operations. The motive is often to show an emotional constituency and faithful donors that a 'generous gesture' is being made. The simple fact of acting implies that 'doing something is good in itself'. Some humanitarians have fallen into this trap. Yet events have taught us that this simplistic short-cut can cause disasters.

When the tools supersede reflection

It is a general observation that the humanitarian community has material, technical and financial means that are outsized compared with its capacity for political analysis and for deciphering its underlying intentions. But the international community presents the same imbalance. As a consequence, the fundamental questions are not asked: should there be wars, and should people die? Is every death unproductive?

Humanitarian morality is not absolute. But who today can define morality? Thus, it falls to the humanitarians to formulate a minimum standard of morality which, in an insidious reversal, ends up justifying their own existence.

Whether they deal with emergency or development, NGOs are confronted with the same questions. In failing to learn from crises, are they not preventing themselves from averting them?

The financial trap

The origin of the funds at the disposal of NGOs either favours or limits their freedom of thought. As the situation in the field is constantly changing, they need the necessary distance and independence to re-evaluate and challenge the validity and quality of the action, to decide whether to stay on or leave. This is impossible if they are beholden to a single donor, or to a political party, no matter how charismatic the name of the department through which the funds are paid out. This applies to long-term projects as well. Without financial independence, periodic evaluations are often biased, as their avowed or subconscious goal is to reinforce the decision to carry on with the action. Without freedom of movement, the risk exists of carrying out actions for their own sake. Capital deriving from funds raised from private donors provides more freedom to manoeuvre.

Some situations bring NGOs face to face with their limits

NGOs, like the employers of civil servants and other international agents, have a rule: not to risk the lives of the people they send into field. This is presently the case in Burundi.

The primary intention is not to abandon the Burundian population to civil war. But what does 'population' mean in a context where armed individuals blend in with the civilians? Who should receive assistance when everyone is a victim and an instrument of oppression in turn? On what level should one respond to very different requests for health care, food, shelter or water for some, and protection and recognition for others whom exclusion, despoilment and violence have cast out of society? Some put all these considerations aside and are mainly interested in revenge. Some groups are ready to sacrifice others to achieve their real political goal: to bring their own ethnically pure group to power, their reference being a genocidal past. In their view, the only acceptable assistance is one that provides them with the means to exterminate the others.

This is the prototype of polarised war which places humanitarian actors in grave danger and makes international aid one of the components in the strategy of conflicting parties: under pressure and threatened, NGOs find themselves restricted to doing that which does not go against the interests of political power.

Events in Burundi are evolving in this direction. The government and the army are trying to separate the population from the guerrilla movements. Against their will, the civilians are gathered together in camps where autonomous survival is totally impossible. International organisations are expected to provide the logistics for water, food and shelter, while civilians who attempt to cultivate land outside the perimeter of the camps risk being assimilated into the guerrilla movements. Likewise, those who do not rejoin the camps that are guarded by the army have their crops burned, their houses looted, or are simply killed. It is obvious that the success of this strategy depends on international assistance. But how does one respond when the government and the army take the entire population hostage and flout the most elementary rules of international law? Who has the power to stop this destructive trend? There is of course public opinion, but we know how passive it was before the beginning of the crisis. And, of course, selective arrangements can be negotiated with local authorities depending on their character but with all the risks that this implies for the humanitarian worker. The *modus operandi* of the humanitarian agencies is not appropriate in such a context. Constant denunciation is sometimes the only recourse.

Burundi is a clear case of a twofold, essential question: can we alleviate total horror? Should we attempt to alleviate it partially?

Notes

1. Adapted from an article in *Courrier de la Planète*, 27 (March–April 1995).
2. M. J. Domestici, *Actes du colloque sur le droit à l'assistance humanitaire*, UNESCO, 1997).

PART II
Combining Skills

Edited by
BRUNO REBELLE

The analysis of crises we have just carried out highlights their complexity and their recent evolution. Consequently, it leads us to question past aid strategies based on a simplistic conception of crisis that drew a clear-cut distinction between emergency situations and development dynamics. We are of the opinion that crises are neither phases of breakdown in the development process, nor passing anomalies in the evolution of societies. They are the result of tensions between certain social groups which, at a given time, have diverging interests. This gives rise to a reorganisation of society, harmful or beneficial, that leaves indelible marks. We therefore implicitly accept that the old dichotomy between emergency aid and support for development must be called into question. This questioning is directed at aid strategies and the underlying motivations of the actors, on the one hand, and at the structures needed to link emergency and development on the other. Then, the possible areas of convergence between these two long-opposed mechanisms must be found.

The findings are clear. Neither development, as the process of evolution of a society, nor development assistance, as an external support mechanism, are guarantees against the emergence of crises. Furthermore, observation shows that emergency aid has difficulty in limiting the effects of crises. And it is also very clear that the constraints of humanitarian action, based mainly on substitution practices, isolate the victims in a situation of dependence in the long term.

Since the beginning of the 1990s a number of crises have perpetuated themselves by significantly modifying their environment: the common themes are regional contagion, growing difficulty in reaching the victims, persistence of survival strategies, and a marked alternation

35

of phases of apparent resolution with phases of acute aggravation of the situation. These elements merge insidiously and it is not unusual to find in the same area groups that are fighting for their survival while others are reorganising their methods of production or their economic activities to take better advantage of the opportunities offered by the crisis. The crisis endures, and yet development is unable to! Thus, emergency aid that was not envisaged as other than limited in time perpetuates itself in the middle term. And development aid that was unthinkable in a crisis situation takes on a new dimension in these particular circumstances.

The rise of the concept of rehabilitation

From the beginning of the 1990s, aid actors and donors have been very concerned by these issues. At first, they confined themselves to traditional chronological analysis. Their thinking concentrated on the interface between the crisis period and the aftermath, when tensions abate and hope for new stability is restored. They envisaged this articulation as a gap that must be filled by means of specific methods, participants and modes of financing. This intermediate phase was baptised 'rehabilitation'. It is difficult to say whether this gap was measured in time – would a certain amount of time suffice? Was it characterised by a specific context that existed neither before nor after, or was it expressed by a specific form of actions – and hence actors?

At that point, rehabilitation appeared as a concept worked out as food for thought for the actors and for the financial mobilisation of the donors. It was not the result of in-depth analysis of the contexts and the practices in the field. It was therefore logical that the term rehabilitation would cover extremely diverse realities and arbitrarily determined time frames.

The NGOs, pragmatic and effective actors, wanted to characterise this situation by giving it a name and designating a set of operative mechanisms. This identification was all the more necessary as the funding for aid made a clear distinction between crisis situations and development aid. This semantic distinction corresponds to a total separation of services and a variety of funding mechanisms. Consequently, funding for activities characteristic of rehabilitation was very hard to obtain.

The Anglo-Saxon NGOs were the first to canvass support for using credits initially reserved for emergency food aid to buy seeds and agricultural equipment to rebuild the production capability of disaster-stricken rural populations as rapidly as possible, during and after the crisis. Their German colleagues then went on to demand that the European Union identify funding mechanisms specifically for rehabilitation. From 1993 to May 1996, the European Council issued regulations governing 'actions of rehabilitation and reconstruction in favour of developing countries'. These regulations follow the direction of the Madrid Declaration adopted at the European Humanitarian Summit in December 1995. It appealed to the international community to continue to make resources available 'to meet the challenge of rebuilding war-shattered societies and thus consolidate a peace settlement and prevent the seeds of future disaster from being sown'. The Declaration also stated that

> The links between relief and development must be strengthened and local capacity to cope must be reinforced. Reconstruction involves not only water systems, bridges and roads but also civil society: the demobilisation of soldiers and the rebuilding of the judiciary and administration and of education and social services.... At the same time, relief must be managed efficiently in order to phase out humanitarian aid as soon as the emergency period is over, switching over rapidly to other forms of assistance.[1]

These initiatives by the European Union, which set up the European Commission on Humanitarian Operations fund (ECHO) for emergency actions, and special lines of funding in the General Directorates I and VIII for development actions, were followed by innovation in the United States, where the US Agency for International Development (USAID) now grants specific budgets to the Bureau of Humanitarian Response (BHR) for rehabilitation and development actions. While adapting to new circumstances, however, these administrations have continued to define rehabilitation as a specific moment in a chronological succession of situations: development / destabilisation / crisis / rehabilitation / return to development. Funding instruments are modelled accordingly, with the consequences in terms of operations that are discussed below.

The chronological sequence is called into question

The excerpt from the Madrid Declaration quoted above invites another comment, one concerning the very content of so-called rehabilitation operations. Here, the mechanical reconstruction of infrastructures (roads, bridges) is placed on the same level as the rebuilding of civil society, although we know that the latter is a very complex process requiring a great deal of time. In this sense, rehabilitation consists in 'restoring the previous level of functionality'. It could have been more pragmatically termed 'rebuilding', in the mechanical sense of the word. In this case one is interested only in rendering equipment, infrastructures and services operational again, generally without taking into account the conditions of their functioning and the expectations of the users. One can see that this interpretation of the concept of rehabilitation is already a source of much future tension. Which trade will benefit from a rebuilt road? Which social group will be placed imperceptibly in a position of ascendancy by being entrusted with the running of a rehabilitated well? The analysis is even harsher when one considers production capacity or basic services such as health or education.

Rebuilding a school is simple, but how will access be affected by changes in the distribution of a population disrupted by crisis? It is difficult to say whether 'rebuilding' a civil society is possible and whether it is in fact a matter for outside intervention. On the other hand, it is certain that the restoration of harmony between the various users of local resources will entail an often long and sensitive phase of conciliation or reconciliation. Likewise, establishing a relationship based on mutual respect between the state and its citizens is an essential and positive process. The preliminaries for the institution of services or the construction of facilities take time, even in the most stable situations. How can one imagine cutting out essential steps in a crisis situation?

All the more so as a crisis leaves nothing unscathed, neither individuals nor their culture, neither their history nor the rules that govern relations between people and their collective or individual relationship with their environment. It is therefore unimaginable that a 'supplementary' emergency intervention followed by a phase of 'reconstructive' rehabilitation would suffice to put things back in order. During a crisis a new dynamic is indeed created, with all the structural intervention that it implies, but especially with human and organisational support combining training, mediation and the restoration of communications between individuals and social groups. It is a long road that leads to 'broader options for the individual and to the reinforcement of community participation'.[2] This is the restoration of the much-vaunted social bond that should precede the reconstruction of infrastructures, and not the other way round. This is where we come up against the impossibility of compressing the time frames of the rehabilitation of infrastructures, on the one hand, and of the reorganisation of civil society on the other.

Observation of the crises that have followed one another in North Mali, and the mechanisms that have been devised to promote a return to normality, show the complexity of restoring normal living conditions, and the impossibility of doing so in a short time. ••

11 • Rehabilitation in North Mali
Variations and Constants since the 1970s
ANDRÉ MARTY

In the space of a quarter of a century, the three regions of Timbuktu, Gao and Kidal[3] experienced three successive disasters: the droughts of 1972—4 and 1982—5, and then rebellion, insecurity and civil war in 1990—5. Each of these upheavals was followed by attempts to overcome the crisis that gave rise to a variety of quite different rehabilitation methods.

Even if the reactions of various actors to each of these traumatic events took different directions — some decided to stay and others to leave, some fell back on traditional know-how while others changed activities and lifestyles, some became more vulnerable and others more secure — it is clear that in the end holistic strategies prevailed. They resulted from local social demand, on the one hand, and on the other from interventions financed from the outside with the approval of the state. These strategies were not the same in 1975, 1986 and 1996, however, even if all went under the name of rehabilitation.

After the drought of 1972—4, emphasis was placed on restoring means of production — livestock for breeders, seeds for farmers, nets and boats for fishermen — and reviving supply circuits by providing basic necessities. These priorities had been confirmed through consultation between the authorities and the farming community. This is how the programme worked to relaunch the cooperative movement throughout the north, headed by the Cooperation Service with the backing of several NGOs, including IRAM (Institut de recherche et d'application). Thus, rehabilitation consisted of reviving the economy through greater participation by the members of the cooperatives and by reinforcing the organisation of the cooperatives chosen as focal points for development in the rural environment. The drought was considered, as much by the authorities as by the farming community, to be an accident that did not challenge the existing production and trade systems.

This analysis was to be revised considerably after the second disaster, in 1985. Drought was then recognised as unavoidable. The objective became, in order to avoid resembling Sisyphus with his rock, to survive as well as possible during the worst years. For safety, it was deemed necessary to organise certain portions of the agro-pastoral land surface. This heralded the advent of irrigated village perimeters, the regeneration of aquatic pastures, market gardening and tree planting, and fixed sites for former nomads.

After the period of insecurity brought about first by the rebellion and then by the retaliation of the regular army, the signature of the National Pact in April 1992 formed the basis for the peace process. This procedure combined emergency and development mechanisms. The rehabilitation linked the restoration of damaged infrastructures with the revival of temporarily suspended or slowed-down pre-existing projects. It concerned schools, dispensaries and administrative buildings in the districts, but also receiving areas (such as wells and shops) for populations that had fled abroad or were displaced within the country and wished to return home.

The term 'rehabilitation' has been used to designate very different mechanisms: the restoration of production and supply systems in 1975; the establishment of secure areas for disaster victims in 1985; and the organisation of administration and receiving areas for returnees in 1993. Beyond these differences the notion of rehabilitation retains its true meaning: 'to restore to working order'. This concept expresses the idea that — following the loss of means of production, of economic or physical security, of infrastructures, of loved ones — the conditions of normal life must be recreated and a minimal level of economic and social viability ensured as rapidly as possible. The idea of emergency is linked to survival, and that of development to a long-term process, although rehabilitation, with its multiple operational components, specifically implies the restoration of human dignity and civil recognition. For that reason, it would be difficult to reduce it to an intermediate space between these two classic forms of aid, as it is in fact an indispensable area of complementarity between the two.

➨ The very definition of the concept of rehabilitation is unclear, as is the creation of specific funding mechanisms. Emergency and development actors, who have acknowledged the significant differences that exist in their respective methods and, moreover, identified a certain number of common values, have long questioned this ambiguity. Consultation has had the positive outcome of bringing their analyses together. Today, both sets of actors feel that it is inappropriate, and even harmful, to establish an additional category of context and action for the management of crises and their consequences. Besides, this compartmenting obliges them to propose different modes of action for each of these virtual stages, creating the risk of an additional dissociation between emergency and rehabilitation, on the one hand, and rehabilitation and development on the other. The concept of rehabilitation as a specific period in time is thereby challenged, practically from the outset.

It is to the Anglo-Saxon consortium ACORD that we owe the first synthetic study rectifying the chronological concept of emergency–development–emergency. The publication in 1993 of the document *Etre operationnel dans la turbulance* (Remaining operational during crises) and of the ACORD diagram marked a turning point in the evolution of this thinking process. This reappraisal is due to the history and the particular structure of English NGOs, which combine both emergency and development sectors in the same agency. Because most of their development programmes in Africa were curtailed or even wiped out by unforeseen, unprepared, crisis situations, the consortium revised all its strategies. In France, this process did not take the same course: there, at the same time, the emergency NGOs initiated the debate. They were having difficulties in 'properly ending an action', or in efficiently carrying out what some tactfully called 'post-conflict technical assistance'.➨

12 ◆ Remaining Operational during Crises
ACORD

Unpredictability and unrest are with us.[4] Crises are occurring everywhere, including in the West where durable growth no longer exists. As for Africa, some contend that the very survival of the continent is at stake. These failures are of direct concern to us as development workers. Our conventional responses, which ignore the risk of crises or are only brought into play after the fact, have become obsolete.

Where development is concerned, new modes of reflection and action are necessary to envisage the idea of change. To remain relevant, development policies must integrate more appropriate means of action in response to an unpredictable and troubled environment. In this respect, several guidelines could be drawn from the theory of chaos management. By chaos, we mean an apparently chance phenomenon that is irregular but recurrent and unpredictable. Drought is an example. It is impossible to predict when drought will again hit the Sahel, but we know that it will happen. Therefore, our inability to forecast a year without rain should not prevent us from preparing for this possibility.

Development

We must substitute a global approach for the European vision of development. An approach that does not require the presence of 80,000 expatriate staff, at a cost of US$4 billion. An approach that does not promote a transfer of Western know-how to the underdeveloped world to bring it up to speed. An approach that takes into account the possibilities for, and the obstacles to development. But whose development? Ours? Development is a process of change for which we require more in-depth analysis.

Change

For many years, the life and social sciences have focused mainly on smooth and predictable change, such as population growth. This is the most easily analysed type of change. But rapid, violent change, such as that which occurs during a *coup d'état* or the sudden devaluation of a currency, is rarely the subject of in-depth analysis, mainly because it is more difficult to evaluate, predict and manage. Unfortunately, most of the problems we face, in particular the development problems, lead to rapid and unpredictable change just as often as they are caused by it. This type of unpredictable change for which it is difficult to prepare presents several characteristics that might help us to understand how we can help populations to face it, and how we can organise ourselves for this purpose.

Complexity

At the root of the real problems is not one single factor, but many interdependent factors. Famine can be caused by drought, a rise in the price of grain, a drop in the price of livestock, inadequate road infrastructures, a lack of food aid, or by all these factors simultaneously. It is not one single factor that is responsible for famine but the combined effects of all the factors.

The 'butterfly' effect

Small changes can have huge consequences in certain situations. For example, it is important to try to understand the events at the beginning of the unrest in Niger in 1990. The organisations had not granted food aid to the nomads recently returned from Algeria. Tension led to demonstrations. The situation deteriorated and finally led to rebellion in North Mali. The small incident in Niger did not cause the rebellion in Mali, but it was one of the catalysts for it. Thus, while this analysis is comforting as it seems to indicate that huge problems can be solved by small-scale actions, it also means that small mistakes can lead to huge problems.

Reacting to the context

Plants and animals adapt and evolve through a process of reactions and, finally, survive changes in their environment. To adapt satisfactorily to rapid and unpredictable change, efficient transmission of the possibilities of reaction is necessary among individuals. With respect to our programmes, this means that our ability to ensure the continuity of our actions and to encourage the necessary reactions is key to our adaptability.

➼ The originality of the ACORD conceptualisation lies in its demonstration that it is possible and desirable to adapt, to varying degrees and to any situation, four types of strategies.

◆ The first set of strategies represent the support activities traditionally associated with 'development' phases, grouped together as aspects of *stable change*.[5] These activities concern income generation, the reinforcement of trade and of local financing capacities (savings and loans), the management of natural resources and the delivery of basic services (health and education). They also concern institutional development and social organisation, particularly women's rights.

◆ The second set of strategies encompass activities that can be associated with the concepts of reconstruction or rehabilitation, termed *transition*. These activities concern political and democratic stability, renewed trust, the safeguarding and revival of production, rehabilitation (mechanical) or creation of infrastructures, training in the broadest sense, reinforcing the ability of social groups to negotiate with their government or with third parties, and striking the new balance in the relations between men and women.

◆ The third set, which address the *threat of crisis*, are aimed at helping societies to prepare better for crisis. These activities concern the development of emergency plans, the organisation of early warning systems, the strengthening and diversification of crisis management mechanisms, the safeguarding of production, the consolidation of the control of resources on the local level, the support of organisational capacity, and the identification of traditional 'anti-risk' mechanisms often operated by women in the domestic sphere.

◆ The fourth set of strategies are more traditionally associated with emergency operations to deal with *acute crises*. These activities include aid (food, shelter, medicines), safeguarding production, strengthening crisis management mechanisms at the local level, protection and lobbying, liaison between affected communities and outside agencies, providing a presence and moral support, acknowledging women's role as protectors of, and providers for the family – all this without creating a state of dependence.

These different forms of aid are complementary (overlapping in some cases) and must be carried out jointly. One should therefore be capable, at any time, of combining substitution, consolidation, development and crisis prevention mechanisms. The dosage of each component will change, depending on the situation in which the actor intervenes. As each situation changes, the amount and nature of the aid and support being provided must be reappraised.

At the *acute crisis* stage, for example, there is a great need for aid to guarantee survival, but it is just as necessary to preserve income-generating activities and social ties. During the transition period, some-times called rehabilitation, the same needs exist but in very different proportions. In situations of *stable change*, activities that support income generation obviously take priority. This does not mean that certain marginalised groups do not receive aid. But this aid is measured in order not to upset the social balance. Moreover, during these periods mechanisms must be developed to prepare for potential new crises.

According to this analysis, enduring war and crisis situations are echoed, in terms of humanitarian response, by actions which closely resemble development programmes and use many of the same tools. Restoring the veterinary services in Somalia, a country with a pastoral economy disrupted by war and drought which led to a veritable humanitarian disaster, will in many ways resemble a development action. This rehabilitation of services will nevertheless be undertaken during the emergency phase. In this context it is the only way to restore a minimum of food security.

This scheme demonstrates very aptly that in almost all situations the four types of support described above should be combined, in varying proportions depending on the circumstances. There is not much point in dissecting the chronological unfolding of a crisis situation. One then speaks of the 'contiguum' approach, based on the coexistence – in the same country, at the same time, and in the same area – of emergency and non-emergency situations. This analysis of the configuration of crisis situations, and of the different types of support that must be combined, has allowed actors to move from the concept of continuum (separation in time) to that of contiguum (complementarity within a context).

Towards combining analyses and capabilities

Based on this new understanding of rehabilitation, the URD group believes that interaction between development and emergency aid at an early stage would foster a better diagnosis and consequently also more appropriate support for the populations affected by crisis. It is clear, however, that this combining of skills is far from easy. The following synthesis of the many debates and observations of the working group – prepared by Marc Rodriguez and François Grunewald – shows the difficulty of joint operational activity, on the one hand, but also points out the areas of complementarity on the other.

Every type of institution has its own culture, its own way of approaching events, its own methods. The various NGOs often intervene on their own initiative, and coordination is rarely a priority. The donors, all with their own agendas, do not really supervise the coordination of the activities they fund. More recently, it seems that budget constraints and the resulting reduction of funding have led to better dialogue, not only between the donors and the agencies, but also between the NGOs. This said, coordination being first and foremost a state of mind, and competition a fact, the pursuit of synergy rarely gets beyond the talking stage and all too often remains non-operational.

The burden of institutional cultures is compounded by the specialised nature of intervention organisms, even if it varies sharply from one country to the other. Anglo-Saxon NGOs are not usually specialised. OXFAM, the main British NGO, created to deal with the refugee problem in Europe after the Second World War, now has departments for emergency, development, development training, lobbying, and so on. This institution could therefore easily combine its diverse capabilities – if each of its different departments were not an island unto itself. In France, there has always been a very clear distinction between the humanitarians, who specialise in emergency situations, the development NGOs, the human rights activists, the lobbyists, and the specialists in non-exploitative economic initiatives. Important changes are nevertheless taking place, and most emergency actors today are also involved in longer-term actions.[6]

The fact that humanitarian action is so strongly characterised by its medical orientation also hampers flexible cooperation between emergency and development actors. This could be at the root of two important tendencies in the analysis of rehabilitation. One puts the victims, as individuals, first and considers the social groups they belong to as secondary. The other extols outside technical aid as the saving element and discounts, perhaps subconsciously, the intrinsic ability of societies to solve crises by themselves. It is probably because the first 'French doctors' originally came from emergency wards, with methods very different from those of the general public health sector, that the concept of emergency aid followed by rehabilitation took hold, giving priority to substitution practices, donations, quick action and the individual.

Yet analysis of emergency and development cultures shows that their respective characteristics are complementary, as the strengths of the one can compensate for the weaknesses of the other.

On receptivity to the concepts of vulnerability and risk

The main strength of the emergency actors is certainly their acute receptivity to the concept of vulnerability. Emergency actors have perfected their ability to identify the most affected and the most vulnerable groups. At the same time, the development actors analyse poverty, describe the mechanisms which produce it … and often give up in the face of the difficulties they encounter in trying to fight it. They gamble on global development as a generator of resources and full employment. Yet we observe, even in our own cities, that development also generates exclusion.

Similarly, the developers' receptivity to the idea of risk is very low, whether it is economic, social or even natural. Once the drought is over, the threat it represents is quickly forgotten and everyone happily readjusts to 'normal' conditions, however temporarily. This relative helplessness in the face of vulnerability and exclusion, coupled with low political awareness, impedes their ability to react to crisis. It disconnects development workers from the concept of prevention.

Substitution or partnership?

The regular return of emergency actors to the same theatres of operation is the result of their unwillingness to encourage endogenous crisis management, making it difficult to take action in the framework of a global strategy over the middle term. This approach to aid has locked the recipients into permanent dependence on welfare. Today, this type of situation triggers new repercussions as the direct delivery of aid to victims is becoming more and more difficult. Expatriate staff and their local colleagues are increasingly threatened or directly exposed to danger, which can cause humanitarian agencies to leave the field in the midst of a crisis. With insufficient local intermediaries, they find themselves unable to pursue their action adequately at a distance. The priority given to logistical efficiency – critical as it is in some cases – leads the emergency actors to do everything by themselves.

Development aid, on the other hand, increasingly puts the emphasis on finding partners in civil society. Barely emerging from a long period during which all its strategies to support local actors were too exclusively focused on state services, it is now looking for other partners to build new alliances. The developers therefore seem to be better armed to prepare local actors to take over crisis management.

Immediate efficiency and middle-term strategies

Concrete solutions, speed, and efficiency are qualities of emergency aid, even if the excessive logistical deployment that results is open to criticism. This emphasis on the operational could usefully be put to work for more durable dynamics if it were supplemented by training and the reinforcement of the operational potential of local actors. This, once again, shows up the limits of an intervention that is too substitutive and too focused on the short term, the immediate result.

In theory, development aims at the middle term, the durability and replicability of its actions. Its own results in this respect are also open to criticism, some of it not unfounded. In any case, it is regrettable that developers require such a considerable amount of time to start up their operations in situations where speed would enable them to take advantage of the opportunities offered by the crisis. Indeed, large-scale mobilisation is possible at the very moment when all efforts are concentrated on getting through an unstable situation.

For developers, however, methodological research has often constituted a priority. Research on working methods has achieved considerable distinction in these circles. In the socio-economic, cultural and technical fields it has fostered the formulation of a range of tools for the purpose of evaluation (ex-ante and ex-post). Rather than perpetuating a simplistic opposition between the emergency actors who are caught up in a whirlwind of action and therefore incapable of foresight, and the developers who intellectualise every move to the exclusion of any actual field action, it would be beneficial to promote common conceptual as well as operational approaches. Analysing the middle-term strategies of development and combining them with the modes of action of emergency aid would certainly be a source of innovation.

Political awareness and political risk management

Humanitarians, by the very nature of their work, confront highly political situations: wars and conflicts, crises that cause massive displacement of populations, or natural disasters during which humanitarian intervention can be exploited politically. The 'humanitarian deed' requires analysis, management and negotiation at the political level. To this end, the emergency actors have devised tools and methods.

For the developers, on the other hand, the political element is part of the environment of their action. They generally attach little importance to the risk of destabilisation generated by this political element. Sometimes, even in the midst of a critical situation, they undertake actions that are likely to exacerbate tensions. For example, interventions that concern the allotment and use of land resources – such as establishing farmers on grazing land – can have destabilising consequences that could lead to a crisis.

On the other hand, developers have acquired a high degree of sensitivity to cultural issues and a great deal of well-informed respect for traditions – whereas emergency actors, by contrast, are regarded as 'bulldozers'. Combining these different approaches to crises and to their contexts could be productive. This would enable a more realistic interpretation by linking political, cultural and social indicators, giving the analysis coherence and relevance.

Bearing witness and sharing

The media exposure which attends humanitarian action is often denounced. Although it is occasionally excessive, one should not neglect the potential educational significance of communications strategies which promote responsible solidarity rather than focusing only on the distressing aspects of crises. It is in this way that development issues cease to be confined to the narrow circles of specialised organisations and the offices of civil servants. They reach a wider audience, reinforcing the necessary sharing of common values and fostering a responsible citizenship that transcends communities and nations.

One of the strong points of humanitarian emergency action, its initial strength in particular in France, is precisely this sensitivity to the defence of human rights, to the encouragement of citizenship and to connecting action with bearing witness. When the humanitarians speak out on these issues, the developers, generally caught up in their economic and social interpretations, sit back and take note.

Consequently, as a result of the rehabilitation concept, both emergency and development actors have begun to upgrade their methods by drawing to some degree on each other's know-how. The following experience of Action Nord Sud in Cambodia is an example of this quest for new approaches to complex situations. Other projects conceived in this spirit will be presented in Part III.

◆◆◆

13 ◆ Rehabilitation in Cambodia: Uncertain Beginnings
HERVÉ BERNARD

From May 1992 to February 1995, Action Nord Sud (ANS) conducted what was termed a rehabilitation project in the province of Battambang in the north-west of Cambodia. In a new context marked by a strong UN presence and the mass return of refugees from Thailand, the term rehabilitation was on everyone's lips. Politicians and donors were in agreement about launching vast reconstruction projects in a country destabilised by years of major disturbances. The NGOs in the field had extensive budgets to conduct rehabilitation projects conceived for massive, quick and visible impact. Accustomed to the traditional dichotomy separating emergency and development, the actors explored rehabilitation as a third option, attempting to confirm that this was indeed a special situation calling for a specific approach.

A special situation

The 90,000 refugees who sought asylum in the province of Battambang found the region in ruins, with neither social infrastructures nor means of communication, and minimal administrative and technical capacity. In the countryside, total reconstruction was needed to attain a level of functioning comparable to that of the 1960s. Returning Cambodians, like those who had stayed on, were profoundly affected by the years of turmoil. Resources to repair the damage, both in human and financial terms, were sorely lacking. This discouraging context was further marked by continuing insecurity due to the presence of Khmer Rouge factions that were still very active in the province. Raids and destruction were common in the villages outside the security zone surrounding the city.

In spite of this sombre situation, the majority of the 600,000 inhabitants of the province asked for no emergency aid for their basic needs: food and shelter. With the exception of a few isolated cases of displaced persons or families in distress, implementing massive emergency aid, food or other, was not justified in this context. Only the floods of 1994 required the local, temporary and simultaneous implementation of emergency programmes and rehabilitation activities. After years spent in refugee camps in Thailand or under the Communist regime inside the country, however, Cambodians needed to recover their autonomy and escape from the grip of permanent dependence.

In addition to residual insecurity and the weak state of the economy, the cruel lack of human resources and specific funding blocked the implementation of genuine, long-term development projects — even though certain isolated areas presented favourable environments for the simultaneous implementation of several different approaches. Finally, heavy pressure from political circles, donors and local populations was driving the various actors to act rapidly for the reconstruction of the country.

A special approach

ANS tried to respond to the pressing need for rehabilitation but did not exclude other forms of intervention when circumstances demanded or permitted them. Of course, the rehabilitation of infrastructures formed the core of the programme in terms of budget, human resources and time. In this field, ANS operated as a contractor, using its own teams to start up operations and then progressively involving technical services and private actors, and providing support for emerging partners. This initial substitution was necessary to enable a rapid return to 'normal', while at the same time encouraging social involvement in the projects, in the maintenance of facilities, and even in the extension and replicability of these projects. This approach also aimed at a high standard of technical quality in rehabilitating infrastructures (metalled roads, permanent buildings). The selection of priority sites in consultation with the population and the authorities was intended to benefit those villages or families which seemed most likely to be able to take charge of the facilities in the future. This approach also sought to boost services that generally fell to the state: roads, schools, health centres. Finally, it was to enable the transmission of know-how: working methods, the drawing-up of plans and estimates. All these criteria were assembled with the single aim of preparing from the outset for the departure of the NGO.

In other fields of action — health, water and sanitation or agriculture — activities were directed either at institutional support whenever possible, or towards supporting private initiatives. These approaches, which are generally the province of development aid, had to be adapted to the context of these transition years. Thus, it was often necessary to substitute for almost non-existent local partners in areas such as the delivery of medicines, agricultural input (seeds and fertiliser) and the provision of essential technical know-how. Large-scale action required the implementation of standardised activities that could be replicated easily by a local team.

ANS endeavoured to render the structures supported by the project flexible and autonomous by avoiding excessive supervision and letting the users themselves take charge of the development tools they had been given: agricultural warehouses, breeders' associations, community health centres, the management of irrigation systems and wells. The systematic participation, financial or material, of the beneficiaries was designed to avoid giving hand-outs disguised as development assistance or promoting empty schemes.

Over-rapid implementation, however, constantly disrupted the emergence and consolidation of autonomous partners. In 1995, ANS wanted to maintain a presence in the area in order to pursue in-depth support work for organisations born of the rehabilitation period and ensure sustainability. But the deadlines set by the donors did not allow it.

This experience taught us that rehabilitation as we understood it in western Cambodia in the 1990s was an honourable compromise. At that time the priority, quite rightly, was to reconstruct and rapidly restore the confidence of the exhausted population. This substitutive approach in which humanitarian actors play the dominant role should be limited in time, however, in order to make way quickly for the traditional national actors. It should lay the groundwork for future development programmes by favouring participatory approaches whenever possible. It should enable the humanitarian actors to rise above their customary understanding of substitutive emergency aid. Far from being a compulsory stage between emergency and development, rehabilitation is similar to a range of tools available to humanitarian actors, enabling them to respond in a timely manner to situations of acute distress that require a rapid return to normality even if some degree of insecurity prevails.

NGOs have thus tried, consciously or not, to combine the roles required in actions such as the fulfilment of basic needs, fostering the development of capacities, income generation and, rather less frequently, crisis prevention. Cross-pollination of the capacities of development and emergency actors must be increased, particularly to promote 'risk awareness' as an indicator for the follow-up monitoring of development programmes and emergency aid.

➤ Intervention strategies
and the obsolete rigidity of funding bodies

Funding is one of the major constraints on NGO attempts to integrate emergency and development. Most NGOs operating in the field of international solidarity cannot cover the enormous costs of emergency or post-emergency operations on their own. The financial support of national, European or international public institutions enables organisations to arrive quickly on the scene of a crisis, to undertake long-term actions, or to work in forgotten areas. The interest is mutual. Indeed, states and international bodies, lacking operational capability, need the NGOs for their speed, flexibility and presence in the field. The funding granted by the donors imposes constraints, however, since its modalities are based on chronological analysis of the impact of a single intervention rather than on an integrated approach.

Quick and high-profile action

The implementation mechanism of rehabilitation projects is open to criticism. It is similar to the management of humanitarian emergencies, and has copied the kit concept of modular intervention, giving rise to the Quick Impact Project. The aim is quick, high-profile action. Supplies are bought and imported, and massive construction is undertaken. Miles of roads, bulldozers digging irrigation channels, brand-new schools and dispensaries are indisputable proof that the international community cares – and not just during the emergency. These actions always follow a schedule established by the donors, the NGOs, and – sometimes – by a state which is regaining its power. They are very often underutilised or, worse, serve as a breeding ground for future tension. This happens because, as we have seen previously, in the midst of a complex crisis situation it is not possible to act quickly and efficiently at the same time. Attempting to rush the resolution of a crisis is probably a serious methodological error and could have a long-lasting negative impact.

A host of examples demonstrate the inconsistencies brought on by this type of strategy. Following this reasoning, building takes precedence over the in-depth restructuring that the ACORD studies have shown to be of prime importance. The experience of Médecins sans frontières (MSF) and of the Comité de coopération avec le Laos (CCL) in Bokeo are excellent examples. ➤

14 • Bokeo: When the Schedule Becomes a Constraint
FRANÇOIS GRUNEWALD

In 1975, tens of thousands of ethnic mountain people from Laos fled across the Mekong river and went on to spend ten long years in refugee camps. In 1992, following the tripartite agreement between the United Nations High Commissioner for Refugees and the governments of Laos and Thailand, they had once again to cross the river and settle in a number of sites chosen by the Laotian authorities. In this case, the European Union's PHARE (Aid for the Economic Reconstruction of Poland and Hungary) programme made rehabilitation funds available to the NGOs who chose to support the Hmong in this difficult phase. MSF, which had worked in the camps at Ban Vinai and Ban Namyo, was involved in the support programme for the health structures of the province of Bokeo. Important work was accomplished to rehabilitate infrastructures, support technical training, and provide facilities and supplies.

Although the intervention was conceived as a health development project, the time frame imposed by the donors was one of emergency. The action had to be rushed in order to meet budget schedules. The first consequence of this was that the operation was carried out mainly in the form of 'substitution'. Training local collaborators would have been more effective in the long term, but takes time. The second consequence was that, while supplying equipment and rehabilitating infrastructures could be done quickly, there was pressure to deliver rapid results in areas that cannot be rushed: in-depth reorganisation of services, the continuity of training activities, and the creation of cost-recovery mechanisms to make the health system sustainable.

The time came when funding for the refugee integration programme waned, the plight of the returning refugees having become a stale issue. MSF was convinced that it was necessary to go on with the structuring and training efforts for a while, so that the project as a whole would endure. It contacted CCL, an NGO which had been involved in this field for over 15 years. A team from CCL and MSF, supported by regional representatives of the EU argued the case for enhancing, through a phase of development, the investments that had been made in the name of rehabilitation. A series of joint missions led to a coherent project corresponding to the expectations and potential capacities of the local Laotian actors. A request for additional funding was presented to the European Union.

Meanwhile, MSF continued the programme with its own funds and recruited an economist to pursue the formulation of a cost-recovery scheme.

In spite of regular telephone calls, volleys of faxes, and innumerable messages left with a variety of departments, Brussels did not respond. Is it impossible to imagine that within a single administration, synergy could be developed to enhance funding mechanisms designed to be complementary? Is it conceivable that budgeting schedules could be separated from the course of the programmes?

For their part, the Laotian actors and their friends in the NGOs despair.

⁕⁕

➻ There is indubitably some confusion between the discourse and the results. As long as 'quick and high-profile' action is sought, the complexity of local situations will be neglected, with the risk that the underlying causes of the crisis-generating tensions one is trying to remedy will go on indefinitely – even though the declaration of the European Humanitarian Summit in Madrid stated that rehabilitation must 'prevent the seeds of future destruction from being sown'.

Harmful chronological segmenting

The idea of rehabilitation as a transition period rules out any possibility of middle-term programming. This period is no longer emergency, defined in units of several months, but it is not yet development, which is programmed in stages of several years. As it is impossible to define the transition from one stage to the other, applying financial mechanisms specific to rehabilitation is a perilous exercise. The result is programming 'by stages', which varies according to the decisions of the moment or to an imprecise assessment of the situation. In Cambodia in 1992–3, rehabilitation was first measured in units of three months and then in units of six months. The rehabilitation plan for Africa – in Ethiopia, Somalia and Mozambique – was scheduled over periods of two years at most!

In such a situation, the operators of these programmes, whether they are local or foreign, have a hard time promoting that sought-after commodity, continuity – especially since the shorter the programme stages, the greater the need for visibility.

Thus, the donors are wrongfully perpetuating the dichotomy between emergency action and development. They are preventing those solidarity organisations which have understood the need for an indestructible bond between the two modes of operation from putting it to work in the field.

The proliferation of channels

Programming is further complicated by the growing numbers of channels that must be addressed by an operator who wishes to carry out an action combining several types of support activities for a population. Although the label put on an action rarely reflects the reality in the field, donors for their part recognise three categories:

◆ *Emergency aid* corresponds to an exceptional situation that justifies substitution by expatriate staff and activities based on measurable results. This requires (1) rapid processing of files, quick decision-making and rapid release of funds; (2) flexibility in drawing up budgets, contracts, and reports; and (3) relative freedom of action for actors whose competence is recognised.

◆ *Rehabilitation* acts on the social fabric and the infrastructures, in continuation of emergency action. It permits the restoration of conditions for resumption of development programmes, in so far as continuity is guaranteed. The rehabilitation programme must be defined in connection with future development activities.

◆ *Development* concerns structuring and training without substitution of staff. It implies giving the NGOs the means to take charge over the long term, with longer contracts and by establishing healthy relations between the partners.

This segmenting requires special channels. But the lack of communication between these channels leads to the excessive segmenting of actions, and hampers them. The case of Mozambique is an example of the difficulties caused by rigid funding structures. That of Kenya, on the contrary, shows to what degree the methods of some actors still reflect the traditional differences between emergency and development. Bosnia is an example of the impossible sequence between reconstruction of infrastructures and social rehabilitation.◆→

15 • From Emergency Budgets to Development Funding: the Assessment of a Difficult Transition in Mozambique
CLAUDE SIMONOT

Like a number of countries undergoing profound change, Mozambique, at the time of the peace agreements, experienced a massive influx of humanitarian aid and development actors, all ready to contribute actively to the reconstruction of the country.

Handicap International (HI) had been on the scene for several years, working as best it could in a complex situation of insecurity and violence. Orthopaedic prosthesis programmes and other activities, mainly in the medical sector, had been undertaken, all funded by emergency aid. These funds had been released by the European Union as an incentive during the phase which preceded the signing of the Lomé agreements.

Once peace returned, the elements of the problem changed. Mozambique, which had become eligible for the European Development Fund (EDF), awaited its entry into the fold of French cooperation programmes. 'There was no longer any question of emergency intervention. No more unauthorised deliveries of food aid, no more hybrid corn to pollute a local agriculture well-adapted to local conditions — no, now we would undertake coherent, well-planned development!' So spoke the donors. As we (HI) had been involved for a long time, and would remain so for a long while to come, we were won over. Renewing the funding every six months, short-term planning — those were things of the past.

On the donors' side, it seems that nobody thought of doing the rounds to assess the actions that had been undertaken before the peace, in order to organise the transition period. At our level, no one had anticipated this transition period or attempted to adapt our requests to the new channels. Thus, the programmes we had established locally, which corresponded to real needs, found themselves, rather curiously, deprived of funding. The emergency had been declared over, and its budget line dried up. New requests for aid were waiting for the first EDF funds to be released, which would take about a year.

A strange situation! Because of our knowledge of the country, the donors requested that we identify very expensive programmes while our own projects, which were small but operational, were cast aside. Was a frenzied race for development projects going to annihilate the modest gains achieved by our actions during the emergency period?

For a whole year, we were caught up in this dilemma and, to prevent the programme from simply coming to a halt, were obliged to finance the project entirely out of our own funds until a link with new budget lines could be established. This was possible for Handicap International, but how many other projects collapsed because of the lack of organisation in the management of aid?

16 ◆ And What if the Problem Were on Our Side?
GENEVIÈVE GUILLOU

In October 1992, Action Nord Sud initiated a programme of emergency aid in Garissa, north-eastern Kenya. The massive influx of displaced Kenyans and Somali refugees fleeing the fighting in their respective countries, and a prolonged drought, required extensive food aid and medical assistance. Several humanitarian organisations — MSF Spain, Care, UNICEF and WFP, as well as ANS — were thus mobilised with the financial support of ECHO.

After several months which were marked by a rapidly suppressed cholera epidemic, the critical period of nutritional emergency was overcome. One after the other, the emergency actors broke off their programmes in Garissa, leaving the nomads as destitute as they had been before this humanitarian interlude. The richest, best-organised shepherds left. The poor ones were unable to rebuild their flocks. For the latter the only recourse was to try to survive on the outskirts of Garissa. This new configuration inevitably gave rise to tensions where land ownership was concerned and to demographic strain.

By 1995, ANS was the only international NGO left in Garissa. In order not to abandon these populations, it modified its programme by offering long-term structuring activities whose beneficiaries would take charge of their own future. It also tried to support local administrations (this change-over had been initiated at the end of 1993). Using ECHO budgets, traditional midwives and health workers were trained in the *bullas*, the hutments surrounding the town. ANS also supported the Ministry of Water in its efforts to improve access to clean water in this area of endemic cholera. In 1996, following through on this initiative, a partnership was formed with the Kenyan NGO Rescue The Nomads to assist irrigated farms.

The reorientation posed little difficulty to the regional diplomatic delegation of the European Union, which approved extension of the funding from the budget line L255-Rehabilitation. The relationship of trust that had been built up over the months with local authorities and the donors enabled the identification of activities and resources suitable for the transition from emergency to development.

Here, the real difficulty stemmed from the relationship that had been established between the NGO and the local population: the latter found it difficult to react as a 'partner' and no longer as a 'dependent'. ANS had trouble getting it across to locals that the role of NGOs is not only to bring kits and 'give' food or medicines. Finally, it was hard to make the transition from the delivery of aid to supporting partners in implementing their own projects. We are convinced that in Garissa the ECHO funding and the constraints that go with it could have been replaced earlier with other budget lines destined for activities involving progressive participation by the population. Accustomed as we are to the automatic renewal of emergency budgets, needing to stand back and assess the new situation but unenthusiastic about the idea of facing complex development budget procedures, we are partly to blame for this unnecessary prolongation of assistance practices.

Therefore, the question is directed at us, the actors of humanitarian aid. What are our real objectives with regard to these groups? Do we wish them to become dependent on us, pleading for our help whenever drought threatens, or do we want to assist them in their efforts to find their own solutions to their problems?

17 • Complex Reconstruction in Bosnia
RICHARD PINDER

The effects of material aid are many, problematic, and impossible to analyse correctly without sufficient time. In practice, reconstruction projects in the immediate post-war period cover four types of scenario: (1) emergency rehabilitation, which means survival; (2) the rehabilitation of collective facilities (hospitals, schools, institutions, and so on); (3) post-war reconstruction to facilitate a return to normal; and (4) the restoration of economic and industrial capacity. These rubrics speak for themselves. And yet, reconstruction represents interests that can cause future tensions if considered only in their material aspect.

The cover of a recent issue of *Courrier International* bore the revealing title 'Schools that teach hate', which sums up the implications of the rebuilding of schools. It underscored to what extent, since the Dayton Accord, the incumbent authorities had, for political reasons, all determined that their reconstruction was a priority — children representing 'the future' as well as a fertile ground for indoctrination. But is that a reason not to have schools?

As for post-war reconstruction, it sometimes follows dubious paths. The reconstruction of private property can sometimes cause envy or resentment. Selecting which houses to rebuild remains the most complex element. As there is not enough time to study the problem, because time is money, this job is often neglected and the assisted population is not always the one in the greatest need. Moreover, the selection depends partly on local authorities, who generally keep some choice real estate operations for themselves.

Taking into account the present level of disorganisation of the government and the degree of corruption which prevails, it is difficult to define a clear limit to its involvement in such an undertaking. However, these doubts should not conceal the positive points. One of these is a project in Dejcici,[7] where the choice of the NGO, Equilibre, and the political interests of the donors coincided.

Whatever the complexity of the problem, an NGO will try to implement projects 'differently', aware that the bonds that are formed during reconstruction are the most important element of social reconstruction. But two major questions remain concerning reconstruction:

- ◆ The first concerns the size of the projects. Is it up to an NGO to get involved in large-scale reconstruction projects, where it will be particularly difficult to do things 'differently'?
- ◆ The second is linked to the cause of the conflict. Reconstruction is sometimes perceived as provocation by the majority when sites are rebuilt for a minority, while the wounds of war are still fresh, on what the majority considers to be *its* territory. In this case, however, not rebuilding means participating in ethnic cleansing.

Everything depends on time and scale: a country is not built in two years, nor can it be rebuilt hastily without adverse effects. Is it the role of an NGO to participate, knowing that implementing large-scale projects in a short time frame will diminish their relevance and could lead to further hostilities?

➙ To give continuity a reasonable chance, we should reinforce the mechanisms of consultation, dialogue and planning between channels in the face of a changing situation, and construct the links likely to influence decision-making processes that are presently too hierarchical and compartmentalised. Such a decompartmentalisation implies a change in mentality – in the NGOs, at headquarters and in the field, and among the entire staff on the donor side.

Competition, duplication: where are we?

The sharing out of responsibility among the various departments of a single donor would be a good thing if it meant a broader array of available tools, of specific and complementary approaches and capabilities. But in practice such sharing out actually leads to division and compartmentalising, as it too rigorously separates emergency, rehabilitation and development when what is needed is flexible communications. All this results in a muddled, certainly not very efficient perception. The actors in the field try to find their way through these mechanisms, criticising their inconsistencies and playing on the prevailing vagueness to gain the resources they need for their operations.

Significant efforts to remedy this state of affairs are being made by the European Commission. On the other hand, the United Nations' specialised agencies do not yet envisage any changes.

NGOs: tools or partners?

Beyond the management of available financial resources and the inconsistencies inherent in the organisation of the various channels that profess to serve crisis resolution, it is advisable to question the nature of the relations between the operational NGOs (emergency, rehabilitation or development) and the donors who massively finance their actions.

◆◆◆

18 ◆ Political Constraints
PIERRE LAURENT

In addition to the structural set-up of the public institutions, there is the question of the political constraints that govern them and, consequently, the roles that these political constraints impose on the NGOs. The Anglo-Saxons and the French share the same view. Their goal is to find a *modus vivendi* among the ambiguities and the opportunities, the manageable constraints, without selling their souls.

Financial constraint is one of the major problems facing NGOs in integrating emergency and development. Most NGOs operating in the sector of international solidarity cannot, solely with their own funds, cover the entirety of their operations; they therefore require public contributions on a national or international scale. Government or international entities such as the French Ministry of Cooperation and of Humanitarian Action and the European Union's Humanitarian Office or General Directorate VIII help organisations to compensate for their own lack of funds in order to work in the long term and in forgotten areas. This works two ways, since governments and international organisations have a real interest in working with NGOs as the latter have capabilities which the former lack: speed, flexibility, presence in the field – in short, operational capacity.

At present, however, these institutions – which we call 'donors' in our jargon – perpetuate a strict conceptual and practical dichotomy between emergency and development aid. The solidarity associations are thus prevented from applying in the field the integration between the two categories of aid which they have accomplished on an intellectual plane. There is no shortage of examples of the absurd consequences of this conflict. How can such absurdities endure?

Systematised emergency action is relatively recent and started to interest public donors in the early 1980s. Development structures, whether bilateral or multilateral, are for their part at least 30 years older. The first drawback thus appears to be age. Beyond changes in judgement or in one's conception of the world, nothing is harder to change than a model of administrative organisation. Positions, situations, careers, habits: these are all structural elements that are seemingly impossible to overcome. Some say that the worst nightmare of politicians is the need to modify the functioning of administrations.

The second drawback is even more significant. These administrations, like any other human organisation, are constantly justifying their fields of activity. In emergency and development, therefore, two cultures, two visions of the world, two very different theoretical approaches are opposed. Mutual accusations of inefficiency have long been the rule. Development is termed useless by emergency structures, which enjoy a legitimacy conferred by novelty and by the 'immediate visibility' of their role in saving from death victims who are supposedly backed by popular support. On the other hand, the developers hold fast to their convictions, all the more as these convictions are constantly being criticised, and deem their own action to be superior because it is sustainable over the long term, and because it gives the beneficiaries autonomy. The quarrel is exacerbated by a considerable increase in funding for emergency actions to the detriment of the development quota.

Yet although its structural and cultural element is sizeable, an administration is only the expression of political will. Beyond the professed objectives of emergency and development aid, the means that governments use are first and foremost instruments of their foreign policy, the strategic interests they contribute to enhancing or preserving. Emergency aid, the darling of the media, confers visibility both at home and in the field, and underscores the solidarity of state X with state Y. Simultaneously, the scale of emergency aid, and the military protection it often requires, make it possible to freeze undesirable changes or political reforms or, because of the crucial nature of this aid, to substitute for governments in beneficiary countries which are often unable to function in situations of crisis. Development aid makes it possible to confirm or introduce conditions *vis-à-vis* the state, to establish areas of influence, but especially to develop areas of economic interest to the donor nation or organisation.

The level of response is subject to these superior objectives of a strategic nature and no administrative upheaval can upset the balance. Foreign policy efficacy comes first, followed by strictly economic interests; then comes – a poor last – the advisability of development and solidarity. It must be emphasised that the major political powers are totally uninterested in the emergency–development continuum. Paradoxically, the only hope today lies with the civil servants who are concerned about the efficacy of their actions and are now discovering the advantages of this link and the complications and aberrations caused by its absence. The road is a long one, paved with trivial problems. The power of the NGOs is to demonstrate, on a daily basis, this natural link.

◆◆◆

19 ◆ Constraints, Strategies and Policies
ACORD[8]

Although the humanitarian organisations declare that their interventions are designed according to the identified needs of populations, in practice there are several factors that determine how they make their choices. They depend partly on the humanitarian aid policies of the principal donor countries and of the UN, on whose political and financial motivations the possibility of NGO intervention to a great extent depends.

For example, without the official recognition of the government of Somalia, the humanitarian organisations were not able to intervene in that country. To whom should they offer assistance? To what extent? How soon and for how long? These are the questions which confront governments and international organisations, and which determine the means put at the disposal of the humanitarians.

If, for instance, official aid to a country is broken off for reasons linked to human rights, long-term programmes under way in that country will be subjected to budget restrictions, worsening the unjust plight of the population.

Let us not be naïve – the distinction made by the donors between 'development' activities and 'humanitarian' activities is more often a function of the political positions of governments than of the requirements of the situation in the field and the options available.

Notes

1. See in Appendix 2 the analysis of these texts presented by the VOICE Consortium.
2. The definition of development according to Edgar Morin in *Terre Patrie*, Editions du Seuil.
3. North Mali, a region of 820 000 square kilometres and approximately one million inhabitants, represents two thirds of the surface and less than 15 per cent of the country's population. It is an arid region with unreliable resources crossed by the Niger River, a vital waterway. The population is sedentary (Songhay, Peul, Bambara) and nomadic (Tamacheq, Maure, Peul).
4. In this document, crisis is defined as a moment when a process of radical change becomes necessary. Thus, a crisis represents a period of transformation or transition threatened by impending disaster.
5. ACORD term for phases of stability, the usual environment for development projects.
6. It must be noted that when emergency actors are involved in long-term programmes, they generally reproduce emergency methods in their development activities: large expatriate staff, take-over and substitution, projects rather than support processes – these are the typical emphases.
7. A municipality of three villages east of Mount Igman, which was inhabited prior to 1992 by a majority of Muslims. In 1993 it was occupied by Bosnian and Serb forces, and the inhabitants fled to Sarajevo. In 1995, when the troops withdrew shortly after the Dayton Accord, the houses were dynamited. The purpose of reconstruction of about a hundred houses was to enable the return of the displaced population to its place of origin.
8. Excerpt from 'Development in Periods of Conflict: Policy and Guidelines', ACORD workshop, 20 October 1994.

PART III
Towards a New Conception of Outside Intervention in Crisis Situations

Edited by
FRANÇOIS GRUNEWALD AND MARC RODRIGUEZ

In the preceding sections, we have shown that disjointed approaches to emergency and development in crisis situations result in gridlock. Crises call for a combination of activities such as free aid or cost-recovery schemes, support for survival strategies, training, education, stimulating production capacity, health, organisational support, and the temporary and sustainable improvement of living conditions together with the security of individuals and property. The level of these activities depends on the need and on the acuteness of the crisis (common types include latent, embryonic, volatile, chronic and recurrent).

The implementation of these activities is constituted by a body of practices in which the donors, the international or local NGOs, technical assistance groups and government institutions are engaged, as well as the local populations and their own organisations. This chapter brings together various reflections on the modalities for implementing these interventions.

The first challenge is to help people to remain alive today and to survive in the future. A population generally does not wait for outside assistance to deliver survival mechanisms. Thus, the preferred method of intervention is to support initiatives already taken by survivors. But supporting local actors represents much more than a simple intervention: it is *the* objective to attain in order to fight the crisis in a sustainable manner.

This first challenge leads to another which is just as important: how to identify the legitimate communities and leaders. Once they have been identified, with which of them should one work? Although the choice of partners is a difficult one, it can be remarkably successful if the partnership is conducted in a mutually transparent and rigorous manner (for example Congo/Zaïre, Somalia, Lebanon). When based on a determination not to discriminate, particularly against highly vulnerable groups (such as women in refugee camps), partnership can prolong an action beyond the acute phase of the crisis and help the actors to take charge of social, and perhaps political, restructuring.

Such partnership is only relevant if it encourages self-reliance and responses that are sustainable in the short and middle terms. Strengthening the driving forces of societies according to principles of solidarity and mutual support, supporting survival strategies, creating the financial instruments to back them up and develop them: all these approaches contribute towards the same goal. But – and this is one of the most difficult problems – the motives which drive the actors of conflicts and the powers that be are quite different from the motives of those who act in the name of solidarity. Bringing them face to face might compromise their respective ideals and means, or even their security. Humanitarian intervention is confronted with the violence of politics. How to act, or not to act, under such conditions?.

Acute crises, and their recurrence, are what every global intervention strategy tries to prevent. And yet, crisis prevention is usually the subject of general debate rather than deliberation on methods of support and financing structures. In situations of latent tension, diplomatic gridlock usually results in exclusion, embargoes, and in the inability of international aid organisations to act, leaving the population defenceless. This is doubtless an area where the need for a real cultural revolution of humanitarian aid is in itself an emergency.

◆◆◆

III. i

20 • Renewing the Modalities of Intervention in Crisis Situations

FRANÇOIS GRUNEWALD

The new approach to the analysis of crises has had a profound impact on the comportment of international solidarity actors. Crisis is not a temporary 'frame freeze' in the peaceful flow of development. It starts well before and ends long after the television cameras and emergency kits have given the event a label. Crisis is part of the process of evolution: the post-crisis period is therefore, by nature, different from the pre-crisis period. What marks the difference between an 'evolution-ary' crisis and a 'humanitarian' disaster is the ability to manage conflicts of ideas or interests by non-violent means in the first case, and the inability to do so in the second case. But the time frame which governs all crises has also evolved. Today, we have a better perception of the chronic or latent character of crises (the proliferation of frozen conflicts), and of the reversibility of most peace-building situations. This challenges the practices of emergency aid (short-term action) and development (which often disregards the risk of crisis). At times when periods of calm and periods of flare-up alternate, and when enduring low-intensity crises set in, efforts must aim at strengthening the popula-tions' capacity to face the crisis and, if possible, helping them to prevent or resolve the next one. Crisis areas are not necessarily uniformly affected. War zones and peaceful zones, active front lines and pockets of stability coexist. A localised conflict can spread rapidly to the regional level. Improving geographical analysis of conflicts enables considerable methodological and operational progress in defining intervention strate-gies according to multi-dimensional parameters.

The need to develop concerted strategies differently

Should the heretofore distinct approaches of the emergency and devel-opment actors be set back to back once again? Of course not. They have all had to progress and revise their methods in order to improve their practices. Now, all these actors must redefine their objectives and methods to integrate their progress so as to improve the quality of their programmes and of their impact – and, finally, to revive the tarnished credibility of both humanitarian action and development.

The present crises require multiform interventions at each of their stages (see Chapter 21). These interventions must be coordinated between the different actors so that one intervention does not ruin the effects of the other, leaving behind time bombs – as can be the case with assistance.

As crises often go on for a long time, they pose two fundamental challenges to the international aid organisations. On the one hand, they should bolster endogenous crisis management and adaptability systems as well as the population's survival strategies. On the other, they should be able to identify and strengthen local capacities – the term capacity being understood to encompass not only trained individuals but also local institutions that can analyse, propose, manage, negotiate, train and lead. These organised structures are often overwhelmed by the scale of the crisis. In that case, they must receive support to enable them to cope with situations of tension and take charge of all or part of the necessary procedures and interventions.

This line of conduct is revolutionary both for humanitarian action and development and for all outside actors. It corresponds only very marginally to their present practices. This is particularly true of French NGOs. The new approach questions not only their methods but their professionalism, specialisation and training. It calls for a redistribution of tasks among national and international NGOs.

Renewing the conception of interventions raises numerous questions

Observing crises

As the first step in formulating strategies, crisis observation today is totally inadequate, especially in the political arena. For the time being, early warning systems apply only to natural disasters. In this area, local intermediaries play an important role as indicators of the social climate. Access to relevant information is a major concern. If information does not flow, analysis is deficient and does not lead to appropriate reflexes in terms of strategy and decision making.

The initiative of the European Parliament in this respect (with the Centre for Crisis Observation proposed by Michel Rocard) might help to improve matters. As far as national and international NGOs are concerned, coordination by countries or territorial task forces must be intensified. This is also a means of promoting prevention, which should be recognised as the result of a better understanding of the causes and determining factors of crises. NGOs which operate during periods of relative calm should include prevention parameters in their analyses and activities, and work towards this aim with local or international specialised institutions.

Supporting survival strategies

Chronic crisis and the sudden outbreak of crisis are part of the history of peoples. Human groups have developed multiform survival mechanisms which adapt to every situation. It is imperative to identify these mechanisms and determine which can be reinforced (such as alternative agricultural production, or the return to family self-sufficiency) and for which alternatives must be sought (decapitalisation, forced overwork). A variety of programmes can be set up in the midst of a crisis to bolster this remarkable form of human ingenuity.[1] For this, the proper tools for observation, analysis and action are necessary. Indeed, setting up such programmes is more complex than importing traditional assistance operations, which are too often standardised.

From project to process

The approach described here gives priority to endogenous and durable problem solving. It no longer favours substitution alone as a 'direct' solution to mitigate the effects of crises; it no longer conforms only to criteria of efficiency and speed. Crisis is viewed in the long term, with its various stages and reversals. The constant of the action during the period of rising tension is based on the reinforcement of the actors' ability to cope with the problems. The English researchers who conceived this approach use the word 'process' in symbolic opposition to the word 'project', which is associated with notions of quantity, time constraints, a lack of planning flexibility, the overweening desire for 'visibility' and the inflexibility of credit lines.

The word 'process' implies several notions, in particular that of a responsible and sustainable association with the local actors. One is with them before, during and after the crisis. Of course, one must have been able to identify, and then helped to reinforce them. The lines of communication must be maintained in preparation for the transition and disengagement periods. A possibility of return, upon request, should be kept open.

This association can lead to projects for which the setting up of traditional humanitarian aid programmes is necessary when the 'added value' of these programmes is deemed to be formative and important.

71

Systematically applying the principle of subsidiarity

Outside intervention should only undertake that which local organisations cannot. When that is the case, institutional support and the development of local actors is the prime objective and applies at all stages of the crisis as well as in a situation of normality. Humanitarian NGOs should seek to form local alliances and support their counterparts, if any. This strategic choice 'to work with and through others' will have an impact on the aid professions. This does not mean that an expatriate presence is no longer necessary. On the contrary, in crisis situations it can have a moderating influence and even participate in mediation if it has recognised negotiation abilities and an understanding for local problems. For that, it must not be perceived as a party to, or a hostage of, the conflict.

Northern NGOs are in charge of a significant share of the international bond

Some aspects of intervention presently cannot be undertaken by NGOs from the South or the East, or by local partners. The coordination of programmes, fund raising, some of the delegated management of the projects, but also international lobbying will for some time to come require cooperation between local NGOs and international participants. What is the place of the former and, most important, how to support their existence? By creating branches of the northern NGOs or simply by recognising their existence? Beyond their institutional implications, the answers to these questions have fundamental operational repercussions, an impact on security, and can even precondition the feasibility of the action.

Is the specialisation of NGOs relevant?

Strengthening local actors to enable them to manage crisis situations cannot be envisaged without an open, multidisciplinary approach. The specialisation of the northern NGOs is rarely favourable to such openness. On the contrary, it tends to exclude certain seemingly peripheral problems. It distorts the way in which the local actors perceive their needs. Certainly, all NGOs cannot be competent in every domain. In this respect, inter-institutional coordination must be achieved.

◆◆◆

21 • Strengthening Survival Strategies, the Key to Intervention
FRANÇOIS GRUNEWALD

Throughout their history, peoples have often encountered difficult natural conditions. By preserving some form of access to food, they have survived. In most cases, 'buffer' mechanisms of adaptation have allowed them to limit the extent of the crisis and avoid the downward spiral of destitution. Strategies for crisis management are the foundations of the three pillars of survival of individuals, family units and societies.

The nutritional pillar of food security

Changing dietary habits (shifting to less and less costly foods: less meat, more cereals; or less cereals, more tubers; and then to survival foods, berries, roots and fruits of the forest, certain types of leaves) constitutes an initial redistribution of available resources. At this stage, the inhabitants of more developed countries rediscover the significance of the family vegetable patch and of small-scale food processing. Adaptive food restriction can, in the long run, lower resistance to illness and thereby lead to a deterioration of the physiological state, which in turn can lead to an increase in the incidence of disease.

The technical pillar of food security presents a wide range of strategies: the use of plant varieties with different cycles and degrees of resistance in order to obtain crops that can withstand diverse weather and plant-care hazards; 'four-legged' savings and insurance in the form of herds or flocks in pastoral and agro-pastoral systems in most of the arid regions of the planet; the development of the wild food resources of the ecosystem (Mozambique, Sudan) that can bridge gaps in food supply; or simultaneous development of diverse ecosystems to limit the impact of weather hazards (Cambodia, Sierra Leone).

The economic pillar of group, family unit and individual survival

Means, often sophisticated ones, are developed to mobilise new resources: temporary migration; the development of new cottage industries or businesses, such as the gathering and sale of forest products, manufacture of charcoal and small-scale retailing; access to loans, often through usury systems or, as in Vietnam and Western Africa, by participating in *tontines*. This is the second level of economic adjustment to the crisis. The third comprises the mobilisation of support in the diaspora, integration into urban employment networks, the creation of women's support groups, and participation in the economic systems of organised crime.

The social pillar of group survival

All of this rests on the cohesion of social groups: collective granaries in the Sahel; the migration through the mountains of entire villages of Tibeto-Burmese in south-east Asia; retirement and mutual pension funds in societies generally considered as developed. 'Not to put all one's eggs in one basket' is at the core of all these strategies, which are often linked in one coherent system. During crises, one observes five stages in the disintegration of this coherence.

Stage 1. Well upstream of crisis phenomena are the anti-risk mechanisms. These are designed to limit the vulnerability of the system to a risk whose frequency has been estimated by the population through its own experience. They are therefore of necessity specific to a place, a region, or a population. It is at this first stage that the strength of the food security systems of the farming community is most evident, especially with respect to natural disasters and weather hazards.

Stage 2. This stage is characterised by adaptation mechanisms that are activated progressively during the crisis in an attempt to check the damage. These systems are well-adapted to low- and medium-intensity crises.

Stage 3. If the crisis goes on too long, or if it directly affects survival strategies, adaptation mechanisms are exceeded. A third generation of phenomena then takes over that gives priority to the social or human element best capable of survival (favouring the long term over the short). The most vulnerable groups sell off their possessions. The weakest individuals are left to die, as they are unproductive.

Stage 4. This stage is one of day-to-day survival. Decapitalisation erodes production. Populations have recourse to strategies that will have disastrous consequences for the environment. Crisis management mechanisms give way to mechanisms of survival in the strictest sense, that in turn eventually lead to the irreversible phase of the crisis, in all likelihood a nutritional disaster.

Stage 5. This is the last stage, during which the body itself 'decapitalises', leading to rapid deterioration of the anthropometrical indicators. It is generally too late to undertake damage-control operations. The only remaining option is food-aid operations, often on a large scale and at great cost.

Understanding this sequence and how a conflict can lead from one stage to the next helps to identify the necessary methods and means.

◆◆◆

III. ii

22 ◆ The Necessity and Specificity of Follow-up Monitoring during a Crisis

Before describing what used to be called 'the two pillars' of the renewal of actions, partnership and the strengthening of the actors, it is necessary to emphasise that organising the follow-up monitoring of an action is an integral part of that action from the very beginning. Monitoring is the process by which the organisation in charge of a project can direct it and change its orientation if necessary. This function is all the more necessary as the situation evolves very rapidly.

Follow-up monitoring is not evaluation

Follow-up monitoring, which is done during the action, is distinct from the evaluation report, which is done at the end of the action. The latter is not part of the operation, it only analyses the result. In the case of monitoring, the purpose is to steer the operation and not only to check, after the operation, that the funds have been used where and as intended.

Following a changing situation is difficult but necessary

Some crisis situations generate very rapid, unpredictable, large-scale changes. In addition to evaluation indicators, observation mechanisms must be used to re-evaluate the material and human resources, the methods and, especially, the overall situation. In a situation of unrest, it is normal for the operators to focus on the immediate. A multi-task 'follow-up monitoring cell' should therefore be created. Its main task will be to establish a frame of reference for risk criteria covering such eventualities as political instability, food shortages and permanent or temporary increases in the population.

Available methodology should not be applied rigidly

Existing methodologies, such as the 'logical process', for example, are of considerable help to operators, but cannot replace common sense, experience, intuition and the opinions of local resource persons. Their sometimes excessive rigidity can even mask problems and preclude

76

caution. This can happen if follow-up monitoring focuses too exclusively on the initial indicators, without taking into account the evolution of the situation and the consequences of actions (see ACORD, pages 78–9).

The indicators

Quantitative indicators (in tonnes, calories, kilometres, etc.) are necessary for basic evaluation itself. They are insufficient for actual monitoring. Moreover, more sensitive 'qualitative' indicators must be defined to identify the breaking points, the moments when it will be necessary to change direction and other key junctures.

Most emergency organisations use methodologies designed to identify the potential security problems that the operators themselves face. Rarely do they question the destabilising effects of their own interventions (the negative impact on prices due to food aid, or the weakening effect on local crops of the massive introduction of seeds unsuited to the local environment), although these must also be supervised and quantified.

Applying crisis indicators to development projects in a 'normal' situation

Follow-up monitoring should take risk into account for development programmes in areas that appear calm but are potentially risky, or in situations of endemic risk. But it never does. The emergency actors rightly criticise this weakness of the developers. The examples of Rwanda and North Mali illustrate the consequences of their oversight.

Clarifying the place of follow-up monitoring in the decision-making process

Follow-up monitoring is a problem when the division of responsibility between operators and donors is badly organised. Power struggles are frequent, especially as the international NGOs themselves sometimes finance the local operators, confusing the situation further. The follow-up monitoring must be organised systematically to play its normal role, which is to allow decision making by the hierarchy. The indicators should be available to all the partners and the temporary and final conclusions debated. These basic principles are rarely put into practice.

The donors must be flexible, too

Follow-up monitoring introduces a necessary element of flexibility into the conduct of interventions. Yet, in reality, the way in which credit lines are imposed by the donors goes against this flexibility. Multiple interests are at stake:

◆ The financial programming forecast is too rigid for the donors (the European Union's ECHO and General Directorate (DG VIII) make provisions for internal adjustments, but their slow implementation obliges the NGOs to go on juggling with credit lines).

◆ NGOs face the difficulty of having to assume the financial burden of programme adjustments (for instance, cancelling a distribution of food budgeted at one million ecus – programmed at the beginning of the action but no longer necessary – means taking a 'loss' of 60,000 ecus for running expenses.

◆ Donors limit the cost of human resources by taking on more or less inexperienced volunteers.

Despite such drawbacks, there is no doubting the long-term cost-effectiveness of a suitable follow-up monitoring system.

◆◆◆

23 ◆ Follow-up Monitoring
ACORD

A strategy of intervention in a conflict situation cannot be formulated without including in the feasibility study a pre-evaluation of prevailing local conditions, and programmes cannot be conceived without follow-up monitoring systems. This makes it possible to have an up-to-date overview of the process, to gain flexibility in adjusting the strategy, and to measure the impact of the programmes. As a rule, the programmes should define clearly how they may reduce or aggravate the risk of conflict.

For example, will material support to the farmers aggravate a conflict over land by legitimising their controversial occupation of it, or will it help to resolve the conflict by supporting the community institutions that settle disputes? Can one begin to distribute material support without first answering this question?

It is important to understand the role of an NGO in this process. Indeed, programmes that attempt to reduce sources of tension and develop capabilities to resolve them before they occur can sometimes produce negative side-effects, bringing to light latent conflicts. In Mali, however, support for institutional development and a large-scale exercise in self-evaluation served as a basis for a whole series of new working methods that were developed during the 1991–2 conflict. In Angola, participatory method-ologies fostered a sense of 'ownership' of the programme, improving security for a time.

III. iii

Partnership: an Operational Attitude and a Philosophy

Strengthening local actors is everyone's objective. It spares having to formulate requests on behalf of the interested parties and overvaluing external perceptions, which often have a destabilising effect. Setting up a partnership is all the more difficult, and must therefore be all the more carefully thought out in a crisis situation. Indeed, emergency situations offer a host of opportunities for taking advantage of the aid bonanza.

However, partnership is above all a philosophy which bestows on the other party the status of actor and no longer that of 'beneficiary-victim'. Imparting to the word solidarity a sense of sharing is not an easy thing in crisis situations. But it is necessary.

◆◆◆

24 ◆ The Choice of Partners: the Naïve and the Ideologists Need not Apply
FRANÇOIS GRUNEWALD

NGOs which support development actions like to begin with collective actions, such as those which involve village or neighbourhood communities and their informal social groups. This grassroots approach is contrary to the top-down practices of governments and experts from the large development agencies. While being attentive to the needs of the populations that are being supported, however, NGOs should not fail to recognise a widespread reality: that the grassroots communities are not homogeneous, and that their organisation often rests on domination and exploitation. These communities, which have emerged from traditional social structures or are based on more recent configurations, are torn by social, economic, political and land-related conflicts.

To involve the population, development actors use two strategies.

The first is to support local authorities rather than the central government and its administration. The second is to stimulate the creation of local NGOs that are totally independent of any centre of power. In all cases, there is a failure to recognise the organisations, such as water management committees, trade unions and organised groups of artisans, that are *sui generis* expressions of civil society and which often have legitimacy and representation.

In situations of conflict, it is even more difficult to identify reliable grassroots partners. Indeed, one of the first manifestations of a crisis is the elimination of those who bear a real message of solidarity. Others are reduced to silence by threats. The organisations with the capacity to act are often decimated or forced to go underground, especially as associating with international actors is dangerous, or even deadly.

On the other hand, the conflicting parties often create their own, well-controlled solidarity organisations. This is a trap. Working with these organisations is indeed effective because, through them, one is sure of reaching the population. But should one support partisan organisations that have no strategy favouring a resolution of the conflict? The problems encountered in Cambodia during the 1980s brought this pitfall to light. These structures are often just fund-generating schemes operated by nationals who know the workings of international aid. Thus, hosts of local pseudo-NGOs appeared in Afghanistan during the Salam operation, and in Somalia and Cambodia in 1993 and 1994. Yet in other cases these organisations promote real social and humanitarian projects.

In their desperate quest for local partners and in the absence of government, a phenomenon which generally accompanies complex emergencies, the large Western NGOs and the United Nations agencies are rarely very discriminating: they are often willing to work with any organisation as long as it is 'local'. Indeed, it is not easy, in times of acute crisis and especially in situations of conflict, to find reliable structures that respect the principles of impartiality, neutrality and independence. Working with structures that are part of the social and economic fabric – women's associations, socio-professional corporations, cooperatives and others – requires considerable precautions to identify the right partners and define the partnership contract.

Formulating partnership contracts

Some may consider it absurd to associate the words 'emergency' and 'contract', and yet it is necessary and possible (see Box 25, pages 82–91).

A flexible, short, revisable contract stating the clearly defined commitment of both parties is part of the operational philosophy that partnership represents. The sharing of responsibility goes beyond the idea of trust, which is necessary but not sufficient.

The contract is physical proof of shared responsibility. It places the partners in a balanced position of collaboration. There is no longer a donor and a beneficiary, but two persons or institutions who have made a commitment. To be effective, a contract should be formal. Whether oral or written, material or moral, it sets down the distribution of roles and responsibilities, and the rights and duties of the partners. It must define the means and methods for resolving problems that might arise. A contract should not be perceived as an inflexible constraint, nor as a sign of mistrust. On the contrary, the joint drawing up of a contract is in itself a collective working process which clarifies the professional, ethical and deontological expectations of the partners and the limits which must not be overstepped. Moreover, a contract helps in the evaluation process: it sets forth the objectives, deadlines, rules and methods. It can be referred to, to measure discrepancies. Finally, it is an instrument for 'painless crisis resolution' if it provides systems of amicable intermediation. Recourse to administrative authorities, mediation mechanisms or law enforcement agencies is only necessary in very rare cases of failure.

◆◆◆

25 ◆ A Project Based on Partnership in an Emergency Situation: Eastern Kasaí, Zaire
MARC RODRIGUEZ AND CLAIRE PIROTTE

This project, conceived in June 1994 by two member associations of the Urgence—Réhabilitation—Développement (URD) Group, is one of the first to bring together operators of different kinds, as well as emergency and development funding right from the start of the action.[2] It serves as the first life-sized operational example, especially as each stage has since been presented and debated before the whole group.

Based on the idea of partnership in a situation of crisis, the project was developed in several directions:

♦ a partnership with the populations benefiting from the action;
♦ a partnership between two types of NGO that usually work in different areas and situations;
♦ a partnership between NGOs and the emergency and development donors which backed the experiment.

Background

In September 1992, inter-ethnic conflict forced 500,000 Kasaïans who had lived in the Shaba region (formerly Katanga, an urbanised mining region) for one to two generations to flee. After an exhausting journey during which many died, NGOs provided emergency assistance, mainly in transit centres. After careful deliberations that went beyond the conventional reflex of setting up camps, the transit centres were kept as temporary structures in order to avoid creating concentrations of populations which, in the opinion of the authorities in this agricultural region, would have been hard to manage.

In October 1993, the situation deteriorated. A multi-agency United Nations report spoke of 'extreme food emergency', but the restrictive conditions for international aid, aimed at putting pressure on General Mobutu's policy, appeared to prevent the release of funds.

In early 1994, in the Kabinda region, where 16,000 new internally displaced persons (IDPs) were arriving monthly, MSF-France managed the transit camp where cases of severe malnutrition were treated as long as their condition required it. As for the others, after a week the families were returned to their ancestral villages without any material aid to help them settle in. When severe cases of malnutrition began to return from the bush, MSF-France asked Epicentre (an NGO) to conduct a nutrition survey in the rural area. It revealed an alarming rate of mortality and morbidity which required food aid. MSF-France, not being specialised in food aid, requested the advice of development specialists within the URD research group in order jointly to set up a suitable project.

Different initial analytical approaches

In the minds of the emergency actors, the idea was to bring in food and distribute it free of charge, after targeting the villages most affected (some had doubled in size) by the arrival of the IDPs, and identifying the worst cases of malnutrition.

Development actors from GRET and from IRAM (representing Groupe Initiative)[3] disagreed with this plan and had a totally different vision of the project needed. First, they noted, the region is an agricultural one:
♦ It is accustomed to exporting its surplus to the city. This capacity

should not be smothered by large-scale, free distribution.

◆ It has two annual harvests. The main period was to begin three months after the survey mission. Therefore, seed distribution was urgently needed.

◆ The land surface suitable for cultivation can be increased and customary law allows land to be granted not only to the descendants of the ancestral owners, but to newcomers as well, though marginally.

The main problem, as they saw it, lay in the risk of a flare-up of tensions between the resident and displaced communities. The numbers of arrivals exceeded the capacity of the communities to absorb them, which explained these tensions, although family solidarity had remained strong during the first months of the exodus.

To give only to the displaced persons was to penalise the residents who had made sacrifices, and thus risk social unrest. To give only to over-populated villages was to discourage those which still had the capacity to absorb more people. As a return to Shaba seemed unlikely, the future of all these people had to be envisaged in this exclusively rural area. The risk of having to absorb new waves of displaced persons was very high, and therefore the inhabitants of the area had to be helped to increase its capacity of absorption.

The area has known structured periods. It still has a network of health agents and agricultural agents who are well acquainted with the situation, traditional local development committees (LDCs) which do not play any concrete role as they have no means, and a religious network which is close to the population.

A participatory conception of emergency action

In view of all these factors, it was decided that the considerable logistical and financial means at the disposal of MSF-F would be combined to address the most urgent need, that of feeding the hungry, but that it would be done in conjunction with actions aimed at helping the resident and displaced populations to become rapidly self-sufficient, thus avoiding clashes between them. The linking of the two approaches is summed up in the idea that 'of course we have to give, but the way in which we do it will be structurally beneficial for the beneficiaries'. Logistics and social stimulation must be associated.

Within three months, in spite of heavy logistical constraints — the state of the roads, the rainy season, the high cost of fuel and transport — the mobilisation of all available actors allowed food distribution to be carried out in a timely and precise manner (during intermediate periods and times of heavy farming). Tools were also provided freely, but seeds were loaned.

This loan was made not to individuals, but to paired units including residents and displaced people, and had to be repaid jointly. This method had the double goal of encouraging the rural residents to teach agricultural techniques to the urban displaced, and to create a small, communal kitty for the village which would serve as a basis for concrete so-called 'micro-projects'.

The mobilisation of all the actors was not limited to the material and concrete aspects of the operation. The project endeavoured to revive the LDCs so that the latter would take on the task of structuring the two categories of population. They were responsible for all distributions and for their fairness, and for all reimbursements. These two clauses were essential for the implementation of micro-projects. They were defined as a result of the priorities chosen by the village as a whole, with the wish to improve the seemingly very basic living standards of both categories of population and give concrete expression to the probability of a common future.

Food, seeds and tools were purchased, whenever possible, in the neighbouring region. The development specialists lacked experience of crisis situations, however, while the emergency specialists were unversed in food-aid problems: as a result, their analyses of the possibilities of purchasing locally were probably not sufficiently accurate. The difficulties encountered in this analysis are described in Appendix 1.

Evolution: two significant periods

INTERVENTION IN A SITUATION OF LATENT CRISIS OR 'A RETURN TO NORMAL': 1994–6

Several months later, MSF-F pulled out their teams as the phase of acute emergency was over. The project continued with the same structure, indirectly reaching a wider population (72 villages, 34,800 individuals). Objectives continued to focus on development actions, and periodic donations and heavy logistics were no longer required. The risk of a new wave of displaced persons arriving from the Shaba region was remote but MSF-F continued to participate in the pilot group and could return if needed. Throughout this period, two types of undertaking emphasised the quality of the partnership:

◆ Micro-projects were not only conceived but implemented by local committees.
◆ Regional activities expanded the capacity for self-reliance.

Only the certainty of being able to mobilise rehabilitation funds from the beginning of the emergency programme made it possible to promise micro-projects and keep that promise. The associations, strengthened by the trust placed in them, gave IDPs and residents an opportunity to work together, with fair representation of both categories. Moreover, the synergy among the LDCs accelerated discussions about land distribution and brought about a lasting increase in the cultivated surface area (the quality and location of the plots occasionally posed a problem). Quite rapidly, the LDCs were prompted to regroup throughout the region: they formed a 'syndicate for the management of farming lands', SIDKA.

The syndicate encompassed 80 villages dispersed over approximately 10,000 square kilometres. By assuming the role of a development agency, it managed the various activities with the aim that eventually they would become autonomous. Its emphasis on self-sufficiency, at least for its own very reasonable structural expenses, started to bear fruit. The syndicate managed tollgates on secondary roads to pay for the maintenance of trails. Eventually its teams of road workers would form enterprises and work on a contract basis. New community treasuries were created every two months and were to be federated in order to manage the villages' funds and their subsidised revenues. This federation was to become totally financially independent of SIDKA in mid-May 1997, according to the analysis of its accounts.

The syndicate was driven by a highly involved community. It was controlled by elected members who on several occasions settled serious crises, especially concerning human resources. The board met regularly; its general assemblies were lively and decision-oriented. The executive body was of high calibre. The syndicate had its own premises, provided by GRET, as well as a plot of land farmed by its staff. It was recognised by local authorities, and the Songhié élite were aware of the advantages the structure represented for them. Good relations were maintained with the administrative authorities and a climate of cautious trust was established in the villages.

Regional activities expanded the capacity for self-sufficiency. Freed from the task of local management, the expatriate and local development actors encouraged the structuring of loan systems in spite of monetary instability, they created income-generating jobs and provided means for road repair and road maintenance services. Since September 1996, GRET has simply been contracting with SIDKA. It controls implementation on behalf of the donors, and intervenes when training or technical support are necessary.

THE RETURN OF ACUTE CRISIS, 1996—7

History, unfortunately, has rekindled interest in the Kabinda example.

In February 1997, hundreds of Hutu families, from the east this time, crowded into Lubao, a large rural community in the administrative sub-district of Kabinda. The superintendent of the town called a meeting of the religious and professional organisations and the general secretariat of SIDKA, which has a link with the outside through GRET, to discuss asylum for these people.

An initial plan was drawn up with two objectives. First, the Hutu fugitives were not to be concentrated in Lubao but kept in the rural areas with the negotiated agreement of the village leaders. Then large quantities of grain, manioc and oil would be procured rapidly through SIDKA, thanks to its widespread presence in the territory and the relations it had developed with local professionals, particularly in the area of transport.

At this point, deserters from the Zaïre army spread through Kabinda, terrorising and looting the population and the shops, creating a climate of general insecurity which extended to the territorial authorities and SIDKA as well.

The outcome

We ourselves doubted the relevance of the Kabinda example to the analysis of crisis situations. When all is said and done, everything went well. Displaced populations were given asylum in their country of origin, with which they had maintained ties. Land, the economic basis for production, was available. In spite of the general climate of insecurity in Zaïre, there were job opportunities for some of the young people in the diamond industry.

But the interest of this example is that it demonstrates to what extent local actors can play an important part in situations of unrest, providing they are organised and motivated to act in the interest of the community. On the whole, the generally favourable development of the project is explained by a combination of factors. Some of these were external: the first harvest was good; there was no new influx of displaced people before the third year of the project; the level of education and motivation among the people was high; the Kasaï region has a tradition of hospitality which was borne out during the events of early 1997. But there were also internal factors: three years on, with the evaluations done, this trial run for 'emergency plus development from the beginning of the action' points up principles which should be retained and new and untested methods which can now be viewed in a critical light (see Appendix 1 for details).

The partnership between emergency and development organisations

In 1994, the joint conduct of an action right from the diagnosis stage was no simple matter. MSF, which defines its mission as acting in situations of acute crisis endangering the survival of the individual, is torn by the debate surrounding the context of these crises and the fundamental question of strengthening the capacity of local actors to cope with crises and manage them. This might entail challenging certain ready-made interventions, and calls into question the professionalism of the expatriate actors.

These difficult questions also arise in the development sector, where development actors have no ready answers. On the contrary, the terms of these questions have evolved since the end of the 1980s and the solutions are still at the experimental stage.

For its part, GRET is an institution which until then had never intervened in a situation of acute crisis or, to be exact, had never analysed the crisis situations in which it intervened. The debates focused on the security problems of GRET's own teams and not on the consequences of the crisis with respect to the conception and objectives of its action. When GRET decided to become involved in the implementation of the Kasaï programme, the decision was far from unanimous and in the end was imposed by the hierarchy. Paradoxically, this decision was taken because of a desire to act quickly and not to retreat from concrete implementation, even if the intervention required a significant portion of donations. The donations were used to create goodwill, to instil trust, and to foster structuring. An unusual combination of speed (in everything including disengagement), direct action and well-managed donations was a feature of the project.

In the field, collaboration was quite successful, with the exception of the occasional personality clashes which are part of the experience. Both cultures reacted in different ways and the project was only completed thanks to the close supervision of those in charge. That there was some conflict was not surprising, considering that the approach was novel for all the participants. Undeniably, all the organisations must overhaul their intercultural technique.

Yet it is not any doubt concerning its validity that explains why so few attempts at this form of action have been made to date, but merely the reluctance of certain executives to invest more time and energy in a significant new field of activity.

The partnership with the donors

This action is a good example because the donors, the European Union and the French Ministry of Cooperation, were associated with it from the start and agreed to the experiment. The risks were great: MSF covered the first two months of food distributions alone, out of its own funds, during which time discussions were held with ECHO and DG VIII. But it is thanks to their joint agreement to the funding of the action over a period of two years, to be paid out as of the second month of the operation, that the project was carried out in the way we have just described. Otherwise, it would have been impossible to guarantee and to structure the implementation of the micro-projects and the development programmes. It would not have been possible, within tighter and more rigid budget deadlines, to adjust to the changing emergency situation and to reappraise the distribution of funds regularly to keep in line with the long-term objective.

For instance, lack of experience in this trial run of the 'emergency plus development' concept meant that two months of deliberation were needed before the decision was reached to cut the number of food distributions initially planned, while increasing the number of beneficiaries. Yet, these distributions represented by far the largest portion of the project. It had taken quite some time to inform ECHO and the services of the European Union were disappointed by the delay, to the point where it became a subject of conflict and acrimonious reproach. Saving 500,000 ecus was considered normal, but the delay in making it known caused a crisis.

The reasons for both attitudes were understandable. The responses that must be avoided are mistrust and fear of sanctions. We know that the most carefully laid plans may be upset by events and have to change course. One must create the opportunity to revise the validity of the decisions with the donors. This is an indispensable and unavoidable condition for the logical working of the whole chain of international aid which must, indeed, be planned and justified but without becoming a slave to management constraints which are often more compelling than the objective to be attained.

Finally, throughout the project emphasis was placed on the explicit analysis of the goals pursued by the operators and the donors, joint concepts that often cover different concrete realities — to save lives, in this case, but also to make life possible by providing the necessary means, and therefore defining the limits of these means.

Conclusion

The conception of intervention that emerged from our joint experience fundamentally challenges not only the emergency practices but also a certain type of development practice. It calls into question the conceptual distinction between the two approaches. It stresses the role of local actors who need reinforcement or help in structuring their work. This objective is relevant in all situations. The modalities of intervention of outside aid must be evaluated in a way that does not stifle the sense of responsibility of local actors in the resolution of their problems. Collaboration between organisations can only be based on this general objective.

Principles of a project based on partnership in an emergency situation

1. Objectives and means are inseparable.[4] Our aim is to reduce the mortality and morbidity linked to food shortage, but to do so using modalities of emergency aid aimed at encouraging sustainable development (or, at least, not hindering it) and the peaceful cohesion of communities.

2. The strengthening of survival mechanisms which have already been set in motion by those primarily concerned. This means:

◆ To avoid offering aid which encourages dependence. If free distributions must be carried out, they should be selective and planned according to the crop schedule. Loans will be granted against contracts guaranteed by joint liability.

◆ To avoid an imbalance in the local economy, which is still active in spite of the crisis.

◆ To respect and reinforce family solidarity and customary law.

3. To avoid the notion of privileged or vulnerable groups — to target only the most vulnerable would have marginalised them. This project endeavoured to help them while encouraging a common dynamic and obliging them to support each other for the common good, as a joint future seemed inevitable.

4. To avoid dissociating food aid and non-food aid during the crisis, in order to avoid dependence. A minimum cash income is one of the pressing objectives. Stimulating the sale of surplus agricultural produce and creating income-generating activities are indispensable in passing from the survival stage to a viable situation.

5. To evaluate existing local resources (such as standing crops, stocks of foodstuffs, possible reopening of markets, availability of transport and tool-manufacturing capacity). This is a difficult yet essential task in unstable environments, especially as speed is of the essence and many factors are hidden. Only this procedure, however, can evaluate the need (or not) for outside aid, and the amount and quality of that aid.

6. To define clear, contract-based partnerships for all the actors. Emergency and development actors, LDCs, the employees of active or inactive administrative structures, local trade unions or NGOs all have a commitment towards the 'project entity' (commonly agreed goal) with the double objective of improving general efficiency and of being an actor rather than a passive recipient.

7. *To make use of the energy generated by the crisis to go one step further, and not to assume that crisis creates only victims.* Hindsight shows us that the entire region has benefited by the know-how imported by these populations of urban origin.

8. *To intervene in such a way that the project is appropriated by those primarily concerned.* It will be necessary to examine the suitability of the proposals and to associate rigorous action (keeping deadlines and promises is essential to building trust) with flexibility towards the actors. The pace of collective structuring, which may vary from one group to the other, must be stimulated but also respected, as it is only this structuring that will guarantee permanence.

9. *To put in place from the beginning of the action a multi-purpose follow-up monitoring cell* (whose role has already been described in Chapter 22).

26 ♦ Partnership and Cholera
PHILIPPE LE BORGNE AND VALÉRIE BELCHIOR-BELLINO

In Somalia in 1994 a cholera epidemic spread from the north to the south of the country. In Mogadishu, security problems made access to the southern part of the capital difficult for NGOs and international agencies. The latter remained stationed in the northern half and took charge of the battle against the disease and of its prevention in the traditional manner: a curative component, with an isolation ward installed in the Karaan hospital by MSF-Spain; and a preventive component, consisting of disinfecting houses and chlorinating wells, which was organised by Action contre la faim (ACF).

For the other half of the city, a cholera task force was created that brought together the Ministry of Health and ACF. A team of sanitation workers and nurses trained to deal with cholera, supervised by ACF, was put at the disposal of the communities. Traditional leaders and NGOs mobilised to create ten decentralised isolation wards in their communities. Responsibilities were shared. The tasks of choosing safe locales, recruiting qualified or unqualified staff, organising the water supply, locating cholera cases, and disinfecting the houses fell to the communities. The task force itself was put in charge of training and supervising the staff, rehabilitating and equipping isolation wards and supplying medicines.

For an equivalent number of patients treated on either side of the city and during the same period, the results of the strategy were better in South Mogadishu.

This can be explained by three factors:

◆ a lower mortality rate due to extensive, early detection of suspect cases observed by local NGOs and inhabitants, as well as safely accessible treatment for the population in the isolation wards located in the communities;
◆ better availability and motivation of the staff recruited in and chosen by the communities (theft of equipment and goods was small-scale compared with that in North Mogadishu);
◆ better prevention of the spread of cholera among the population, which understood the disease and reacted appropriately.

The difficult security conditions in the southern part of the capital led to an original approach to the cholera epidemic that brought better results than the traditional strategy used in the north. Good relations and a climate of mutual trust between the communities and ACF led to the rapid organisation that enabled the population to take charge of its problems and keep alive its ability to deal with cholera.

27 ◆ Finding the Right Partner: the Same Problem for Northern and Southern NGOs
ELYANE COMATY-MITRI AND BÉRENGÈRE CORNET-VERNAY

The war in Lebanon received extensive media coverage in France: expatriate humanitarian organisations went to Lebanon and mobilised a great deal of money, and the Church exerted a certain amount of pressure on French Christians to support their brethren there. In a situation of this type, northern NGOs seek the collaboration of local organisations, more often in search of efficiency than out of a desire to establish a genuine partnership.

To reach the victims as quickly as possible, southern NGOs were used as a bridge or even left out altogether. They were often used only as subcontractors. More than 2,500 organisations saw the light during the early years of the war, of which many were connected to religious communities, sectarian groups, political parties or even militias. Faced with this diversity of local organisations, although some were of long standing and experience, how to find the right partner in the south? And what would be the defining characteristic of this partner — docility?

The war plunged Lebanese NGOs into a new situation: until then they had been few, operating mainly in the socio-educational sector, and now they were proliferating, most of them improvising emergency aid programmes. Local associations were badly disorganised and confronted with an influx of outside intervention and funding, while before the war they had been used to relative autonomy thanks to national funding.

At the same time, the victims had to be reached as quickly as possible and these NGOs often seized upon the means offered by outside organisations without making too many conditions or demands.

The conditions for effective partnership

Although they were not acquainted, the Mouvement social libanais (MSL, Lebanese Social Movement), and the Comité catholique contre la faim et pour le développement (CCFD, Catholic Committee against Hunger and for Development) shared points of ideological convergence: to resist sectarian conflict and act for the population without discrimination, and not to remain stuck in the aid—development dichotomy. There was also methodological convergence, in considering populations first as actors rather than mere beneficiaries or victims and, towards that end, creating structuring actions rather than mass distributions.

How to act when the conflict drags on?

When a war drags on it creates its own momentum and moves from one place to the other. Zones that are disaster areas one day might be normal the next. This even engenders a kind of 'addiction' of the population to war as a condition for survival. During 17 years in Lebanon fighting and peaceful periods alternated and may continue to do so, as events in the south in the spring of 1996 reminded us. This pendulum movement is typical of this kind of context, which swings in disorderly succession from maximum emergency throughout the entire territory over a period of several years, to absolute stability.

Partnership after emergency

The purpose of partnership is continuity. Yet, as soon as the media lost interest, the humanitarian action disengaged massively and abruptly — although the transition from war to peace is a slow and fragile process, as Operation 'Grapes of Wrath' reminded us. Peace is a process in which civil society plays an essential role through tolerance and understanding towards others. Supporting organisations born of civil society during this fragile phase must remain a priority.

Finding the right partner on both sides

Partnership is a two-sided relationship which must be based on trust, harmony (which does not necessarily mean a similarity of opinions) and cultural exchanges. But partnership also means rigour and transparency, which guarantee the efficiency of the action as well as accountability both to the donors and the beneficiaries. The terms of the relationship must be defined by contract.

Finally, it is during the post-emergency phase, when the guns are silenced but the country remains to be reconstructed, that the quality of a partnership can be measured. Although the work of some of the actors is then over, for others — those who have found the right partner on both sides — it goes on, towards a civil society which must be organised to face new challenges.

28 ◆ The ICRC and the National Red Cross and Red Crescent Societies – a Very Special Partnership

CARLO VON FLÜE

Since the mid-nineteenth century the relationship between the International Committee of the Red Cross (ICRC), the various National Red Cross and Red Crescent Societies and the latter's umbrella organisation has been one of both complex internal chemistry and momentous outside developments.

All run on the basis of voluntary service. The 170 National Societies form a unique world-wide network that cooperates with the ICRC in both peace and war. The motto of the International Red Cross and Red Crescent Movement, whose work is based on a set of fundamental principles, is *per humanitatem ad pacem* (through humanity to peace). Cooperation between the ICRC and the National Societies is stepped up in periods of tension. Those societies enable the International Committee to take a broader range of actions and in return receive support that makes them better able to meet the vital needs of the population before, during and following a crisis.

This special partnership presents obvious advantages, particularly in terms of logistics. And the National Society can often facilitate ICRC work by helping it adjust to the local culture and by explaining local problems. The fact that the Society is active in the country before conflict breaks out enables it to set up support systems for the civilian population well in advance, and its active presence may become decisive should security problems restrict the presence of foreign nationals. The National Societies also help to ensure that emergency programmes take into account long-term concerns.

But there are difficulties as well. For example, National Societies increasingly find themselves serving as agents for other bodies, especially United Nations organisations, which ask them to implement their programmes as the Societies are frequently the only appropriate organised entities in the area. This certainly improves the coordination of field work, which is always desirable, but executing programmes designed by governmental bodies is sometimes difficult to reconcile with an approach based on the fundamental principles of the International Red Cross and Red Crescent Movement (set out in Appendix 4).

Similarly, in situations where humanitarian actors must deal with forces recognised neither by the central government nor by the international community, the National Society is often unable to take action, and officially unrecognised Red Cross or Red Crescent Societies may then be set up, using former branches of the National Society as their basis. The ICRC may agree to work with these organisations even if they are not in a position to respect certain principles, such as that of independence, but efforts are nevertheless made to enable them to act in accordance with the ICRC's principles. It is sometimes difficult to combine effectiveness, long-term presence and neutrality, but a world-wide local network is often the only means of ensuring ongoing development despite crises within the local organisation. A common set of ethics and a clearly defined partnership are the key to ensuring that the relationship between the national and international organisations remains one of complementarity.

III. iv

Strengthening the Actors, or Helping Them to Strengthen Themselves

Crises lead to a redistribution (or strengthening) of the roles of the various actors and groups in a society and often to a change in the organisation of the economy. Some are always losers, however, regardless of their degree of involvement in the conflict. Women are among these groups, as victims of cowardly warfare that has resulted in a proliferation of areas infested with anti-personnel mines.

◆◆◆

29 ◆ Social Differentiation between Men and Women in Humanitarian Interventions
JUDY EL BUSHRA

Although the international community has made progress in the field of emergency action – increased speed of reaction, targeted interventions, fostering of social awareness – it too often neglects the particular needs of women, and sometimes even contributes to diminishing their status.

Although the social differentiation between men and women transcends differences relating to material wealth, age groups, occupation or ethnic groups, it contains areas of specificity:

◆ the immediate needs of women in emergency situations;
◆ different forms of subordination of women;
◆ the role of women in reconstruction and reintegration.

Awareness of these specific problems makes it possible to improve the efficiency of emergency intervention in the short term and, in the longer term, the capacity of all the communities to rebuild themselves.

The immediate needs of women

The speed and extent of changes brought on by crisis situations affects the position of women, who must often provide alone for their children and families. It is essential to help them preserve their physical, psychological and sexual health, and above all to protect them from violence aimed directly at them.

The physical safety of women is often threatened in situations of lawlessness, when they are the targets of violence and rape, and when fighting takes place near inhabited areas, marketplaces or farmed land. For example in Cambodia, Somalia and Angola, anti-personnel mines kill or maim a large proportion of women. Handicapped for life, they often receive only limited aid as artificial limbs are reserved for professional soldiers. Unable to carry out their domestic chores, they are often repudiated.

More than half of households are without men during conflicts. They are missing, have joined the fight, are seeking jobs, or have been taken prisoner. The stable population is then usually made up of women, children and the elderly. It thus falls to the women to devise replacement strategies when food is being used as a weapon, by interrupting supply lines, preventing access to fields, or destroying stocks.

As for health, the needs of women increase in emergency situations. Besides the absence of paediatricians and gynaecologists, they receive no help to overcome the psychological traumas they are subjected to, such as assault, rape and unwanted pregnancy.

Different forms of subordination of women

The subordination of women in society explains why they have poor access to resources and to decision-making bodies, and why they are the targets of physical assault and abuse. Men control the resources and decide how they will be used and distributed, not only at the level of the household but at the level of the community. Women often do not have any possessions of their own (land, livestock) but are also deprived of intangible benefits such as literacy, higher education, and hence information or contacts with organisations. In a crisis situation, with little representation on the local or national levels, they are often at a disadvantage when food is distributed by emergency aid. Mass rape by militias is often used as a deliberate, organised humiliation strategy. Refugee or displaced women are therefore in particular need of protection.

But tension periods also occasionally contribute to reinforcing the inferior status of women within their own communities when the identity and integrity of the latter are threatened. The rise of religious fundamentalism and the tightening of controls over women – their behaviour, activities, power and freedom whether or not to procreate – are all elements of this identity crisis.

Women nevertheless spontaneously tend to become involved in the peace process. In order to carry out her daily chores, a woman must maintain contacts with the enemy in crossing front lines to go to market, or in trying to preserve her marriage if she belongs to a community which is opposed to that of her husband (as is the case for many women in Somalia, for instance). Moreover, women are highly sensitive to the effects of war on those around them: raped daughters, outcast mothers, grieving parents, missing children.

Social differentiation between men and women and the reconstruction process

International aid can meet only a small portion of emergency needs, and represents 10 per cent at most of the total demand. The survival of the population depends more on its own capacity to work at income-generating activities than on the distribution of food or other aid. In practice, this means the capacity of women, as the survival of a community depends to a large extent on their efforts. Supporting women in times of rapid change or disaster lays the foundations for a reconstruction or rehabilitation process.

Indeed, disasters bring about fundamental changes in the relations between men and women that can lead to permanent change with potentially positive or negative effects.

Changes in the distribution of work

Distinctions between the roles of men and women recede in times of conflict, when women take on responsibilities which formerly devolved on the men. After crises, men, who have a hard time readjusting to civilian life, are also confronted with a different domestic balance that aggravates the process of social disintegration. Thus, in Uganda, international agencies have taken it upon themselves to facilitate dialogue at the community level in order to redefine the relations between men and women in a way that is acceptable to all, thereby contributing to social reconstruction by taking all aspirations into account.

Changes in the perception of marriage and the marital relationship

Because of the high death rate among men and the experience they have acquired in times of crisis, some women decide not to return to the social position they occupied prior to the conflict. This independence profoundly modifies the state of motherhood. It can impel some to enter into recognised or unrecognised polygamous relationships which offer only limited protection and material support.

Women retain considerable cultural influence

◆ The education of children places women in a position to influence the behaviour of future generations.

◆ Women can incite their companions to seek revenge, compensation or settlements to which they are not entitled – or, on the contrary, can prevent them from doing so.

Thus, conflicts and crises impel women to organise themselves for their protection, to promote their interests and discourage violence. Specifically supporting women's organisations can help them take charge of their own destiny, and can help the whole community to recover after the crisis.

Recommendations for the conception of emergency interventions

Disasters provoke upheavals but they also shed light on hitherto neglected forces and resources. The status of women is one of these. Failing to recognise and fully support their contributions and role can marginalise them and diminish their status further, squandering a wealth of talent and energy that is essential to the reconstruction of the community as a whole. But defining the situation of women is a difficult task because they are generally confined to their households and hard to contact. Hence, this task cannot be undertaken lightly. To be relevant, it must take into account several parameters, which are:

◆ to involve the affected communities and in particular women in the preparation of emergency aid plans, their implementation and follow-up;

◆ to respect the views of the local communities, including women, and to elicit their capacities and technical skills;

◆ to build up the capacity of local organisations and in particular women's organisations that can benefit the entire community;

◆ to address both the immediate problems through timely intervention, and the long-term needs;

◆ to recognise that, finally, the measure of a successful intervention is in the positive, long-term impact it has on the community as a whole.

These key principles are valid for all international interventions, whether they are for emergency, rehabilitation or development. The distinction which is generally made between the three has proved of little use. The decision makers, practitioners or politicians, would do better to break down the barriers and retain the best elements of each approach in planning their activities or funding. Agencies should avoid static emergency programmes and invest in research, planning and consultation jointly with all the beneficiaries, men and women, using active participatory methods. These strategies will make it possible to take more appropriate and efficient action, and enable communities to face future upheavals with greater confidence.

◆◆◆

30 ◆ The Specific Problems of Unaccompanied Women in Displaced Persons' or Refugee Camps
ANNETTE CORRÈZE INTERVIEWED BY CLAIRE PIROTTE

Camp conditions are difficult for all women, but particularly for unaccompanied women.

A census of women heads of families
Following the departures or deaths of their husbands, many women find themselves in unofficial or multiple relationships. Few are recognised as heads of families, yet widowers routinely have this status. The consequences are serious in terms of access to aid distributions, especially of tools. Why not regularly update the initial census when staff are in daily contact with the camp population?

The organisation of camps and the specific needs of women
The lack of mobility of women with many young children constitutes a serious handicap that threatens their own survival and the survival of their

children. It renders any kind of access difficult for them, whether it be to nutritional centres, to the distribution of food aid or to firewood that must be gathered far away. Difficulty in finding work in the area of first asylum is aggravated by the competition of men and adolescents, who enjoy more freedom of movement.

It is not easy for an unaccompanied woman to find someone to mind her children. The staff of humanitarian organisations can bear witness to a decrease in solidarity due to frequent absences. Are those in charge of the camps, along with the women's groups and existing networks, trying to find ways to set up small, reliable income-generating projects?

Safety and medical protection problems

Unaccompanied women are especially vulnerable to violence in general, and sexual harassment in particular, because of overcrowding, forced idleness, social customs that sometimes give male relatives of a widow rights over her and the proximity of armed elements that can lead to sexual pressure or rape. The consequences are predictable in terms of pregnancies or sexually transmitted diseases.

Should contraception and gynaecology be envisaged by emergency actions? 'Yes,' say the humanitarian workers in the camps, 'but emergency kits are not designed for this.' Neither are facilities available to women who are forced by adverse circumstances to seek abortion. Should emergency kits not be re-examined?

These questions may seem trivial in view of the scale of the Great Lakes crisis, but they are real and solutions would be easy to find.

31 ◆ Finding the Last Anti-personnel Mine: an Emergency for Long-term Development
BILL HOWELL

Even when the main infrastructures have been cleared and sensitive areas de-mined, mines remain scattered about the fields, the watering places and the outskirts of villages because these areas are rarely considered priorities on a national scale. De-mining cannot be envisaged solely in terms of emergency and outside military technical support. It determines the entire future development process of a country, with the twofold advantage of increasing the availability of land suitable for cultivation and decreasing the risk of accidents.

Specialists from the United Nations and other international organisations recommend the total elimination of mines. But costly commercial contracts are not possible in all cases. It will take years, even generations, to reach this objective. Therefore, it is not a case of simply setting up emergency programmes, but of working for the long term. Furthermore, because of the slow progress being made in de-mining, political interest and financial backing may wane. It therefore appears essential to develop local capacity to deal with the problem of mines in those places where they are causing the most damage to mainly rural populations. By close consultation with local leaders and taking into account existing initiatives and the motivation of the administrations and decentralised authorities, it should be possible to develop long-term de-mining capability for the villages according to their needs and resources.

To be effective, a de-mining programme must be integrated on several levels:

◆ it must be an element of any humanitarian assistance or development programme;

◆ the fundamental principles of development must be integrated into any de-mining programme, both at the planning stage and in its implementation;

◆ the government must take full responsibility for integrating effective de-mining programmes with all its other activities.

Generally, a state of emergency, the insistence on bilateral solutions and a lack of funds lead to the establishment of a centralised agency of doubtful sustainability. An alternative approach must be sought. The partnership concept, which has proved cost-effective and promoted the emergence of local capabilities in other fields of action, is a concept which is directly applicable to the de-mining issue. The advantages of decentralisaton, of a communal approach and of progressive development of local technical capacity can be applied to local de-mining. In the end, moreover, local governments can gain politically from this type of activity as it addresses directly the needs of citizens, with a positive effect on the sustainability of the programme.

III. ʋ

32 ◆ Using the Money in Crisis Situations
François Grunewald

During humanitarian crises, recourse to exogenous (loans) or endogenous (cost-recovery) financial resources is the subject of much debate:
Is it ethical? Is it feasible? What does experience show us, taking into
consideration the fact that a lack of interest in economic matters often
explains the recurrence of tensions?

Credit and loans in times of crisis

The considerable difficulties encountered in setting up micro-credit
programmes in peacetime become formidable indeed in a crisis situation. Yet they remain the appropriate tool for such a situation. Whether
it is for 'sophisticated' farming with its diverse requirements, or for
urban economies with their numerous informal micro-activities, this
type of programme is well-advised and viable. Helping the actors to
meet their own needs thanks to micro-credit can be an appropriate
solution and have a leverage effect.

Although important work has already been accomplished in stable
(Bangladesh, Senegal, Ivory Coast, Nepal) or relatively stable (Laos,
Cambodia) situations, there are still few examples of credit programmes in crisis situations. One knows only how complex they are to
set up and the general rules that must be observed: the setting of credit
ceilings in the experimental phase, the importance of establishing
contracts, the advisability of systems of joint liability rather than
material guarantees or mortgages, or the application of interest rates
that take devaluation into account. Experimental programmes are
being carried out in the field – in the former Soviet Union or Zaïre, for
example – and are being monitored to assess the value of this powerful
tool, micro-credit, in situations of latent or acute crisis.

Monetising aid

The principle is simple: since free distribution has numerous negative
side-effects, the beneficiaries must be made to pay for the aid they

receive. Prices are usually subsidised and therefore well below those of the market, which are themselves inflated by scarcity and speculation. This makes it possible for populations impoverished by crisis to cover their needs without decapitalising and without becoming accustomed to free aid. One of the first experiments in monetisation of aid was carried out by the ICRC in Hungary between 1956 and 1958. The usefulness of such programmes depends on the degree of decapitalisation of the population. During acute food emergencies, families are often unable to pay even subsidised prices. Later on in the crisis, maintaining low prices by means of monetisation programmes can have a demotivating effect on farmers. Indeed, at that point, everything will be expensive, but with the price of grain maintained at a low level, remuneration for farming work will also be very low. Demonetisation programmes are therefore of interest in pre-emergency phases (to prevent decapitalisation) or in post-emergency phases (to prevent dependence).

In each case, many factors must be taken into account which influence the setting of prices, including current labour costs, the standard of living, the fluctuation of demand and the mode of functioning of trade networks. This is not easy. Almost all the food aid monetisation programmes set up in Somalia by NGOs working with the WFP failed. Nevertheless, the European Union is still experimenting with food aid monetisation programmes in the framework of the TACIS (Technical Assistance to the Community of Independent States) programmes. In countries that are switching to market economies, it is a matter of setting up private grain trade networks. These experiments remain to be evaluated but early results show that the theoretical model of 'injection of food aid/monetisation/reviving of the private sector' does not always work.

Moreover, monetisation programmes include setting up 'counterpart funds', provisioned by income generated by the sale of the product of aid goods. This income is then reinjected into assistance programmes – a process that can lead to numerous further problems. Indeed, the money generated can represent considerable amounts in comparison with the budgets of the ministries of countries torn by civil war or shortages.

Cost recovery

Participation by the population is also the aim in the financing of cost-recovery programmes. But in this case, rather than constituting a commercial transaction, payment for services (medicines, hospital care, veterinary supplies, seeds) enables the creation of working capital. Thanks to this capital, the community can replace the stocks sold. The experiments being carried out in many countries following the 'Bamako Initiative' show the interest and the difficulties of this approach. The participation of the population in the running costs of health structures and the purchase of the medicines they use implies the availability of at least a minimum of cash. The destitute or, more generally, populations living in crisis zones which are usually very impoverished, are often incapable of contributing to the cost of the health services they need. In Mali, a lot of groundwork was needed to adapt this policy to specific conditions in the northern regions that were in rebellion. The principle of 'partial rather than total cost recovery', particularly concerning the cost of infrastructures and logistics, was accepted in early 1997.

Trade

Humanitarians in general are very reluctant to use economic mechanisms. Such means seem incompatible with the ends, and the risk of perversion is high. From the 'charitable' standpoint, trade is seen as enriching a few and impoverishing those who are already weak. The reality, however, is much more complex.

Some economic actors are also victims of conflict. One has only to observe the endless small businesses that crop up in and around the camps for refugees and displaced persons. Since aid generally provides a limited variety of goods, the beneficiaries sell part to buy what they lack. The sale of wood, the manufacture of charcoal and the marketing of forest products are often a main source of income for the populations of cities and their outlying areas in times of war. In Somalia, Angola or former Yugoslavia, micro-retailing flourished at the height of the crisis. It facilitates 'divisibility' (the sale of goods in minute quantities to those who live from hand to mouth) but leads to high prices (each middleman takes a cut).

These observations are incentives to work in collaboration with carefully chosen actors. An instructive example is that of Somalia where the ICRC has recently been using the existing economic networks to supply the hardest-hit areas. There is admittedly a price to pay to the tradespeople who take the risk of buying and shipping food and seed to unstable areas. But the price of a ton of goods which is actually distributed is less than that of the same quantity bought, shipped and distributed by an international agency. An additional advantage is that the goods come from the country itself: rather than going into the coffers of European or American producers, or others in neighbouring areas that are not affected by the conflict, these purchases contribute to rebuilding the local economy.

The fact that many of these programmes fail is no reason to give up. Analysis of these mechanisms and the know-how required to make them work still remains to be elaborated. The key factor which is lacking in emergency situations is time: time to identify the modalities best suited to the situation, time for training and, especially, time to explain. In any case one must remember that the longer the period of free aid, the more difficult will be the transition from free aid to partial participation in costs.

At the outermost bounds of material aid: the myth and reality of Food for Work

Food for work (FFW) programmes designate food aid which, instead of being distributed free of charge, is used as payment for work destined to stimulate the creation or maintenance of collective infrastructures such as irrigation systems or road repair units. They can also aim at preventing natural disasters through techniques such as the construction of anti-erosion barriers, terracing and reforestation.

The conditions for the success or failure of this type of programme are relatively easy to identify by means of an economic calculation similar to the 'calculation of the cost of opportunity' for the use of available labour. When food is scarce and therefore expensive, and job opportunities are few and badly paid, FFW becomes attractive. This has been verified by the WFP in certain countries affected by severe food shortages, and by certain OXFAM irrigation programmes in Cambodia. Interest fades as soon as other options appear or the daily wage in other sectors is higher than that offered by the FFW programme.

In the ICRC programme to relaunch the manufacture of agricultural tools in Afghanistan, the blacksmiths requested payment in kind, then in cash, then again in flour, according to the fluctuations of the war, the price of grain and the regularity of supplies. Moreover, local labour must sometimes choose between farm work (tilling, sowing, tending the fields, harvesting) and non-farm work (house repair, woodcutting, handicrafts) on the family farm, and the opportunity offered by 'food for work'.

Thus, the programming of FFW activities is sometimes simply impossible. In the last analysis, despite all the justifications, it is illusory to offer a FFW programme when the differential in remuneration between FFW and regular wages becomes too great. It is therefore necessary to evaluate FFW remuneration according to local salary scales and job opportunities.

One area in which FF W is nevertheless effective is the maintenance of traditional collective structures. Here, the wealth accumulated by certain strata of the population, particularly in the form of stocks of grain, is partially redistributed through work which benefits the community. In Afghanistan, FFW corresponded to a traditional form of organisation of labour. In payment for the maintenance of the *karezes*, underground irrigation systems, the water lords – the owners of these systems – redistributed a portion of the taxes to the poor farmers. The workers were fed. When war led to the decapitalisation of many families, everyone struggled for survival and this maintenance work was no longer done. FFW has revived this practice.

Finally, in certain cases, FFW is used to subsidise states or institutions that can no longer pay their civil servants or employees. Such practices could be justified in contexts of conflict or immediate post-conflict and near-total economic collapse: no more money, no food in the markets, extremely low wages compared with the price of staple foods, and so on. One must nevertheless be careful not to perpetuate these programmes as an easy way out. Certain examples show that the side-effects of this system can be disastrous in the long term.

Food aid and regulation of prices

Programmes to stabilise prices through food aid operate according to a relatively simple system: when there is a surplus one buys to prevent the producers' prices from collapsing; when there is a shortage, stocks are released to prevent prices skyrocketing and the risk of social crisis (food riots usually accompany price hikes, especially in urban centres). Although they are satisfactory in theory, such programmes encounter many problems:

1. They require integrity on the part of the institutions which stabilise prices. Under the conditions prevalent in many countries, this body (often the national grain bureau) is sometimes subject to great pressure and its executives are exposed to temptation.

2. The cost of warehousing (rental and maintenance of buildings, management of the stock and, if necessary, regular fumigation and other services), destocking and rebuilding reserves is heavy. There

are technical problems: Europe went through this experience in 1970–80, when its grain and milk surplus was damaged by mould and rodents.

3. These programmes are often hit directly by the cost-saving measures recommended by the International Monetary Fund (IMF) and the World Bank. Based on the principle of state intervention in the market to stabilise prices, favourable both to producers and consumers, these programmes go against the laws of supply and demand and free trade. They are therefore prime targets for the Bretton Woods institutions.

In this field of activity, the real problems are actually related to the fact that reserves are often built, not with local produce, but with imported grain produced in the north. Although the second part of the equation – lowering prices in times of shortage – can be realised thanks to these imports, the first part – supporting the local economy – cannot.

With little incentive to produce surplus goods, therefore, farmers turn to autarky and stop producing goods for sale. The urban handicraft industry that lives off the transformation of these goods is also ruined. The vicious circle of food insecurity in the cities begins, although the potential of local production is not utilised.

◆◆◆

33 ◆ Emergency Aid for Income Generation
ACORD

From the outset of acute crises, some interventions are carried out with a view to development. The conventional criteria applicable to credit and cost-recovery systems are not always appropriate for areas affected by conflict. The economic situation is such that income or loans are used for survival. The difficulties encountered by the debtors can lead to irregular reimbursement, causing a mediocre rate of recovery and hence a decapitalisation of the funds loaned. Occasionally, rather than keeping to traditional credit systems, which in fact transform loans into subsidies, other types of support should be examined.

In Juba, South Sudan, for example, ACORD switched from a system of supplying tools and seed on credit to a system of advance payment. The project introduced more profitable crops and allowed the farmers to release funds to pay in advance, in cash.

Interventions such as supporting savings and loan groups, setting up systems which combine loans and subsidies, or supplying tools to the local markets, can be just as important as credit. Any system, especially if it has been devised in a period of crisis, should identify from the outset the capacity of the target group to ensure the repayment of the loan and, consequently, determine whether it is subsidies or loans that are in order to fund the planned activities. One should avoid conceiving unprofitable economic programmes for aid purposes.

34 ◆ Economic Solutions: a Difficult Concept for Some Emergency Operators

Myanmar is ruled by a strong military regime. It is composed of federated states populated in the centre by Burmans and in the east by Tibeto-Burmans, and the state of Rakhine, populated by a majority of Rohingyas who came from Bengal, probably in the fifteenth century. British colonisation prompted migrations in the nineteenth century, whose consequence today is that the Rohingyas are not recognised as Burmese nationals, no matter how long they have lived on Burmese territory.

In 1978, 250,000 Rohingyas refugees from Myanmar were settled by the High Commissioner for Refugees (UNHCR) in Bangladesh. In 1979—80 they returned to Rakhine. In 1992, the scenario was repeated and, since 1994, UNHCR has again organised a repatriation.

The analysis by UNHCR of the causes of the exodus recognises that the reasons are essentially economic. The state organises the corvée, which is compulsory for all — construction of roads, bridges, and other public works including Bhuddist temples — and which can go on for several weeks, without pay. A very high proportion of the Rohingyas live off unstable daily jobs and own no land. If they accept the corvées they very rapidly find themselves without any resources to live on. When they have nothing left they must flee.

As of 1993, specialists in agro-economics recommended to UNHCR a twofold action to resettle the refugees durably: the construction of vital infrastructures (such as sanitation and schools); and the organisation of economic development programmes (loans, changing certain farming practices, and other initiatives). UNHCR retained only the construction of infrastructures targeting local populations, without tying this develop-ment work to national projects. This action did not address the economic reasons for the exodus (except as it affected a few marginal groups such as widows).

In August 1996, 10,000 people fled. UNHCR requested that NGOs submit proposals. Their solutions were similar to the previous ones: planting a second crop, small loans systems, and a coordinated plan to permit sus-tainable actions by putting the beneficiaries in charge of their own development. UNHCR agreed and went ahead with the operation. It simul-taneously organised free, emergency-type distributions without any co-ordination, however, which vitiated the overall project.

This case illustrates how problematic it is to take into account the economic factor in contexts that are allegedly emergencies. Attempts to obtain a lasting reduction in the number of refugees fail because they do not take into account the reasons that caused people to leave in the first place. They also illustrate the importance of a joint approach to an emergency action that is necessary and high-profile, and therefore often material, and of collaborating over how that aid should be given. This is a condition of bridging the gap between emergency and development.

Notes

1. Ways to stay alive today, to survive tomorrow, and to gain a foothold in the future are developed in Chapter 21.
2. Medécins sans frontières, France (MSF-France) and Groupe de recherches et d'échanges technologiques (GRET).
3. Groupe Initiative, a consortium of French development NGOs composed of CICDA, CIEDEL, CIEPAC, GRDR, GRET, IRAM, SOLAGRAL and VSF.
4. A representative of the World Food Programme said, 'We must first break through the con-ceptual wall separating emergency and development.'

PART IV
Open Debates

Entitling Part IV 'open debates' could lead the reader to suppose that all the ideas presented in parts I–III are no longer the subject of debate. Far from it. It simply underscores a shared interest in continuing, together, to challenge practices and modes of analysis. Among the many questions to be considered, we have selected four.

1. Crisis prevention: must one attempt to prevent crises in the sometimes illusory hope that one can actually stop them from breaking out, or would it be more appropriate to focus first on limiting their effects on those populations that are most vulnerable?

2. The diverse ethical and deontological visions that animate the actors of international aid. Should one, because one is working in a situation of crisis, abstain from public denunciation to preserve access to populations at risk or, on the contrary, should one bear witness as a primary means of action to protect the victims?

3. What are the relations between NGOs and public authorities – between NGOs and the states or bodies of states that finance the actions, but also between NGOs and the host countries? What should be the relations with legal authorities, guerrilla movements, destabilised regimes? The NGO does not come into an uninhabited area, and should remember, on leaving, that its stay will leave a lasting imprint on existing social relations or on those that are being rebuilt.

4. Finally, the open debate which as yet has hardly been explored deals with the nascent relations between humanitarians and the military. In light of the changing nature of today's conflicts, these relations are becoming more common and pose serious problems.

Our first contribution to this debate (page 150), written by Philippe Truze in 1996, sketches the general panorama of situations where military and humanitarians meet in circumstances where their area of competence and mandates are clearly different. The second article (page 154), written by Véronique de Geoffroy in 1998, analyses the specific and relatively recent types of roles that the military take on during rehabilitation phases. At the core of the evolution of the actors, of their motivation and of the contradictions that have been observed, this point opens a complex but urgent debate which interests Western countries as well as UN agencies and NGOs.

◆◆◆

35 ◆ On Trends and Their Effects
FRANÇOIS GRUNEWALD

To 'sell' a project to a donor:

◆ 20 years ago one termed it an 'integrated development project';
◆ 15 years ago one spoke of 'research–development';
◆ 10 years ago: 'women and development' and 'popular participation';
◆ 5 years ago the indispensable reference was 'sustainable development';
◆ for the past two years the 'emergency–development continuum' has been the formula to attract funds.

And today, 'prevention'?

IV. i

36 ◆ Different Aspects of Crisis Prevention
BERNARD HUSSON, ANDRÉ MARTY AND CLAIRE PIROTTE

Obviously, one can hardly attempt to prevent a crisis if one doesn't understand it. But beyond this necessary understanding, crisis prevention poses problems for NGOs that a debate on the articulation between emergency and development cannot disguise. Indeed, it is advisable to define carefully what it is one wishes to prevent and to think through the best approach to use.

◆ Prevention can take on an unhealthy aspect if it consists only in pointing the finger at certain groups, instilling the idea that there is only one acceptable way of thinking.

◆ The prevention mechanism must be accepted as legitimate by the whole of society. Particularly if mediation is requested – and all the more so if it is not spontaneously requested – the legitimacy of the mediator is an important factor for success. This legitimacy rests on recognition by the parties to the conflict more than it does on the standing of the institution. Multilateral or international bodies are therefore not necessarily in the best position. Intervening on their own initiative does not guarantee results for international organisations , either.

◆ Negotiating skills are required to carry out a preventive action. In a crisis situation negotiation cannot be improvised. This type of negotiation requires precise *savoir-faire* based on previous experience.

Questioning prevention

Although prevention stems from worthy intentions, it is often called into question in some of the ways discussed below.

Where to draw the line between interference and prevention?
In the name of what values can a preventive action be carried out? Where does one draw the line between interference and preventive

action? Can there be unanimous agreement on undertaking preventive action?

At what point should one intervene when the level of tension indicates a threat of conflict? And who should decide on the moment of intervention? The experience of the past few years shows that these difficulties are of a political nature rather than related to the formulation of criteria for intervention.

Prevention can have negative side-effects

Information that there is clear risk of crisis in a certain area can have the effect of decreasing the aid that area receives. The organisations in the field, which quite rightly do not wish to endanger the lives of their representatives, may reduce their support or even stop all aid. Thus, in the 80 areas identified by the United Nations as having tensions that could rapidly evolve into crisis situations by the end of 1993, precautionary measures resulted in the unavailability of international institutional assistance to develop internal defence mechanisms and consolidate negotiating capacity.

Conversely, if a permanent preventive mechanism existed, the parties to a potential conflict could fuel tensions in order to benefit from preventive measures, particularly financial aid, and to gain political recognition.

Publicity versus discretion

The simple fact of announcing that preventive action is envisaged can have considerable impact. It is advisable to act with extreme caution. Therefore, when a country is threatened with internal conflict, prevention cannot be carried out overtly. But this creates a complication: if prevention must be a discreet process, on what authority can a potential agreement be founded? Who will rally round this process outside of a small circle of leaders?

The publicity versus discretion issue is also a problem when there are, *a priori*, no political interests. Accordingly, in the case of a food shortage, the government often delays announcing it as long as possible, until well after international warning systems have forecast the impending crisis. Indeed, it is always a delicate matter for a state to have to declare publicly a deteriorating domestic situation rather than announcing progress.

Different forms of prevention

Although trying to prevent crises is not without merit, the important thing really is to fight against the marginalisation of social groups that have no other recourse than violence to make themselves heard. This choice leads to a number of questions:

◆ Do we want to turn development into a strategy for crisis prevention? In that case, development must be defined as a means of social regulation rather than as a means of increasing the resources of the destitute.

◆ Do we want to act to prevent latent crises? For this type of mediation, which is a long-term process, states and international organisations are better equipped to act through diplomatic channels than are NGOs.

◆ Do we want to avoid the eruption of a borderline situation into full-blown crisis? In that case, it is the framework of dialogue between the parties that must be maintained.

◆ Is it a matter of preventing the deterioration of an ecological environment that is a potential source of humanitarian disaster? In that case, protection of the environment, seismological and climatic research, or agronomic warning systems are the appropriate tools.

◆ Do we want to spare the victims the consequences of crisis – by acting to prevent the unavoidable conflict from causing avoidable suffering?

The answers to all these questions are varied and cannot be codified. Isn't the real issue not to try to prevent crises but to limit their impact?

Limiting the scale of crises

Once a conflict appears unavoidable, the task of damage control falls in part to the outside organisations present in the field, and particularly to national and international diplomatic bodies. But, confronted with their shortcomings and poor organisation, NGOs find themselves obliged to direct their actions towards five areas that have also been identified by the emergency and development organisations:

◆ They must develop diagnostic ability to prevent human tragedies. NGOs make every effort to use multidisciplinary teams composed of agronomists, nutritionists, sociologists, economists, legal experts and political analysts in order to formulate accurate diagnoses. Their experience of the field and knowledge of the context are indispensable advantages in containing conflicts.

117

◆ They must develop analytic and early warning capacities. Crises are always preceded by warning signals. In Rwanda, Cambodia, Somalia, Ethiopia and Peru, information was available. In the case of Burundi, it was broadcast. NGOs need this information in order to alert those in charge. Whether they are specialised in prevention matters or not, they must constantly keep the political authorities informed of the situation, as is presently the case in the Great Lakes crisis. Indeed, the vast majority of conflicts occur where they are expected. Zaïre is an unfortunate but telling example.

◆ They must maintain a state of permanent preparedness. To this end, two actions must be conducted jointly: developing familiarity with the available resources in the areas adjoining the zone of potential conflict, and training competent staff on the spot within the intervention organisations, during the pre-crisis period.

◆ They must facilitate dialogue and trust between potential or overtly hostile belligerents. These actions may concern such matters as 'neutralising' hospitals or the safe passage of convoys. Thus, certain agencies, particularly the Anglo-Saxon ones, specialise in organising discussion groups among the civilian population.

◆ They must organise coherent support for crisis management mechanisms. In the areas of food, agriculture, sanitation and supply, a number of activities to contain the impact of a crisis on the population can be undertaken very rapidly if they have been planned early enough.

In the field, certain development agencies have a tendency to procrastinate – empty promises, indecision, unproductive discourse, repeated postponement of the intervention – with the very harmful result that the population is under the impression that nothing is being done to support its own efforts or, worse, that aid is being misappropriated.

Prevention, which in certain cases is reduced to 'disaster preparedness', is an area of which we have little experience at present. And yet, the evolution of conflicts and increasingly difficult access to the victims make it essential to reconsider the methodology of prevention.

◆◆◆

37 ◆ Better Utilisation of Early Warning Systems
FRANÇOIS GRUNEWALD

Presently, several systems are in operation at different levels:

◆ The global system of the UN's Food and Agriculture Organisation (FAO) covers the entire world.

◆ FEWS (Famine Early Warning System), a system developed by USAID, works at the regional level.

◆ Other systems operate at national and sometimes even local levels.

Some of these systems mainly use data furnished by satellites, others use only climatological and agronomic data. Their usefulness is generally very limited.

The most efficient systems without any doubt are those that combine information from different fields, including the social sciences, particularly the analysis of price curves and economic phenomena such as unusual sales of livestock or irrational activities. Using this approach, the ICRC is setting up its own early warning system which, in addition to analysing data from FEWS and its related systems, is based on a network of regional delegations that continuously take the pulse of potential crisis zones. A regular comparison of the map of areas with unstable food and economic situations, and of that of high-risk areas with geopolitical, inter-communal tensions, would seem to give a reliable indication of intervention.

But, of course, these crisis detection systems are only of interest if early warning results in quick action.

◆◆◆

38 ♦ Burundi: When Material Aid Is not Enough
JEAN-EUDES BEURET

The sudden occurrence of emergency situations occasionally leads development organisations to participate temporarily in emergency aid according to an approach characteristic of their existing relations with local actors.

In October 1993, the Burundian crisis caused massive population displacement. In the absence of actors specialised in emergency aid, Opération d'appui à l'autopromotion (OAP) was asked to help.

In an emergency...

From the start, OAP put a great deal of effort into implementing a system to help the victims take charge. Each group of displaced persons, whether in sites or dispersed, chose a committee to carry out a survey of needs and specific problems, and to take care of distribution. Community relays were formed, composed of representatives of the administration, the Church, the victims' committees and of resource persons with a personal commitment recognised by all. The function of these multi-ethnic bodies was local consultation and they served as intermediaries between OAP and the committees when insecurity hampered mobility.

These bodies were not just the transmission belt of an action that was beyond their own capacities: they were our partners and they participated in the conception of the overall emergency operation. Beyond the survival of individuals, it was a matter of preserving the dignity and responsibility of people, as well as the existence of moderating bodies and social action to fight against the destructuring of society. In the same spirit, dialogue was opened with the victims in order jointly to arrive at an understanding of the dynamics of the crisis; early on, the victims had indicated that their need to understand was a vital priority.

Facing the diverse polarisations in Burundian society

Impeded by a shortfall in human resources, the task of activating these bodies was all the more difficult to carry out as for months it was necessary to defend the action and the local intermediaries against the forces of polarisation in Burundian society. Ethnic polarisation existed in the administration, the Church, and between the educated élite and farmers, and there were continual attempts by this élite to manipulate the committees. In a situation of institutional destructuring, these committees were rapidly perceived as a political bargaining chip to be used to regain lost credibility and screen the politically all-important flow of information in order to control the unstable, ill-defined, displaced population by masterminding the aid.

Maintaining the balance of power that guaranteed joint control within the committees and community relays required a great deal of effort and only proved effective in the long term as the result of constant pressure. It is therefore illusory to imagine that these committees and local intermediaries could be totally autonomous: almost everywhere, this would lead to manipulation by local authorities involved in the Burundian conflict.

Frustration...

OAP quickly realised that it was powerless to deal with the local dynamics of the conflict, although at certain precise moments there were ways of curbing certain aspects of its development. A conflict always evolves in stages, both physical and psychological.

In retrospect, one of these concerned the openness of the various parties to dialogue. At the start, the victims had high expectations of communicating with other victims from different ethnic groups, in order to understand the violence many of them had been subjected to or had themselves inflicted, often without understanding all its implications.

Exchanges between displaced Hutus and Tutsis were encouraged in consultation with the local administration that supported this approach, but did not take place, lacking the agreement of the foreign cooperation partners who objected that humanitarian aid and conciliation actions do not go hand in hand. From that point on, each ethnic group withdrew unto itself and its suffering, giving its history a unilateral slant that would give rise to widespread mistrust — dialogue became impossible, an almost irreversible boundary was overstepped.

When local actors wish to take the step towards dialogue, should one call in 'reconciliation specialists' — of which there are so many at the national level, and so few at the local level? Should one wait for tempers to cool down? It was up to the actors present among the population who were known to be neutral to encourage dialogue while there was still time: they proposed activities to organise the different population groups, supplying material aid but also an opportunity to discuss the future together. Now, we can only regret this lost opportunity.

IV. ii

Ethics and Deontology

If there is an aspect of emergency that concerns development actors, it is certainly that of the ethics underlying the choice of actions. There is more than a subtle difference between impartiality and neutrality: on what basis would an international law be decreed that would 'legitimise' intervention?

The articles gathered in this section are deliberately contradictory and interpenetrating. They are not intended to demonstrate the superior merit of one theory or the other but rather the scope of the debate and of the difficulties that must be overcome to maintain solidarity actions in prevailing circumstances.

◆◆◆

39 ◆ Humanitarian Assistance Is a Right
PIERRE LAURENT

Humanitarian assistance is a right that has been formalised to some extent, in part by the Geneva Conventions and their additional protocols, and in part by a gestational, ongoing process in the Security Council of the United Nations, as proved by certain of its resolutions. It is thus a fundamental right that proceeds from the syncretism between the conventional, the customary, and jurisprudence. It is the right and the duty of each individual and of all to give humanitarian assistance, the right of each individual and of all to receive assistance in distress. Although this right is, in itself, incomplete, all the legal instruments exist for the protection of humanitarian bodies and their free access to the victims of conflict. In practice, two factors circumscribe their use:

1. The first concerns the permanent and systematic deceit of the signatories to the conventions, who continuously violate them. The new shape of conflicts during these last years of the twentieth century

only aggravates these violations. Opposition movements, minorities, guerrilla movements and militias in open conflict with the authorities in their countries do not feel bound by the signature of the government they oppose. Conflicts conducted by criminal organisations and plunderers who are not identifiable political actors fall outside the framework of conventional negotiation. How can one apply the law to them?

2. The second stems from the fact that the Geneva Conventions only apply to wars or conflicts recognised as such. Yet humanitarian assistance is necessary in other situations as well: dictatorships and totalitarian governments in which populations are at risk (Chile in 1973, Poland in 1980, North Korea and Algeria today).

Restoring priority to international humanitarian law, particularly to allow direct access to the victims, implies above all updating the formalisation of this law which integrates the changes imposed by the practices in the field. The conservatism of legal experts, as well as the opposition put up by those who consider themselves guardians of the law, are partly responsible for holding up progress. The controversy of these past decades, particularly concerning the right to interfere, is not just the pet theme of a few actors. It reveals a political commitment to adapt the law to new international realities. There is an urgent need to reconcile the law of Geneva with that of New York, to develop a single body of humanitarian law which encompasses assistance and retributive justice for crimes against humanity, including genocide.

This revision is too serious a matter to be left only to the legal experts. The humanitarian actors, born of civil society, have the duty and the legitimacy to carry out intensive political lobbying. Whether their authority is the result of political polarisation since the Cold War or whether it is the result of the political will of enlightened men and women, it is up to these individuals – who may consider themselves as above not the state but the reason of state – to shoulder this responsibility.

But there can be no application of international humanitarian law without means of sanction and coercion. Formulating the latter is, however, a difficult enterprise. To get around it, many have seized upon the latest fashionable concept: conflict prevention. Obviously, it would be simple, and so much less costly both in human and financial terms, to intervene before crises break out. But several recent attempts compel us to realism and pragmatism: the risk of disillusionment is great. First of all, beyond the fact that wars are sometimes necessary, it is utopian to believe that the countries of the North will sustain a durable interest in poor countries that do not present major geopolitical or economic interests. Furthermore, prevention is very low-profile as far as public opinion is concerned. Media pressure discourages politicians from taking this direction. Finally, as one observes in the most advanced democracies, repression and sanctions are preferred, irrationally, to prevention. Therefore – as we foresee in the near future neither a policy of prevention, nor a real commitment on the part of states to institute, through international bodies, a policy of solidarity independent of special interests – we must support a policy of sanctions. The violation of the right to humanitarian assistance should be punishable under criminal law and therefore constitute a criminal offence. The criminal courts for the former Yugoslavia and Rwanda have opened a breach that we must use to make progress in the formulation of permanent jurisdiction empowered with adequate means of enforcement and independent of political influence.

It is a major ambition, but no more daunting than that which compels us to help fellow human beings in distress, no matter where they may be.

◆◆◆

40 ◆ Assistance and Protection: Implementing International Humanitarian Law
Carlo von Flüe interviewed by Claire Pirotte

Few situations confront the individual with greater danger than does war. But alleviating the suffering caused by armed conflict is of little use unless that action is accompanied by a firm and formal undertaking on the part of the leaders who cooperate with it. And those leaders are often responsible for having started the war. In any case, action in response to conflict should not be taken in isolation. Efforts to prevent conflict are essential and must be stepped up.

In 1864, the ICRC initiated the idea of creating a body of law that would be applicable universally in the event of armed conflict – *jus in bello*. The result was international humanitarian law, today subscribed to by virtually all states in the world.[1]

This law has developed steadily to take account of modern realities.

Originally designed to protect sick and wounded military personnel and the medical staff responsible for their care, its scope has expanded to cover all persons not (or no longer) taking an active part in the conflict (prisoners of war as well as the civilian population). The Protocols additional to the Geneva Conventions, adopted in 1977, provide minimum guarantees for all victims of conflict, whether international or not.

Born of war, it is in war that international humanitarian law must make its voice heard: how can the destruction be limited? How can regular troops or other armed groups be persuaded not to violate the law, as they all too often do? How can the suffering, particularly of the wounded and the sick, be alleviated and civilians and their property protected? How can a measure of humanity be maintained in wartime? How can moderation be ensured in situations where force no longer knows limits, where violence and arbitrary action have the upper hand?

International humanitarian law does not say 'Do not make war', it makes no claim to prevent conflict from breaking out. What it does say is that even in the extreme situations constituted by armed conflict not everything is permitted. This law is applicable and must be respected by all warring parties, both perpetrators and victims of aggression. Above all, the law of war in no way makes war more acceptable; it merely offers a degree of protection against the effects of conflict. It does this by banning attacks against the civilian population and by prohibiting starvation and forced displacement as means of warfare. It provides for the protection of all the items essential to the survival of the civilian population: food supplies, agricultural areas, harvests, livestock and drinking-water installations. Protocol I protects cultural property, places of worship and the environment; it outlaws all attacks on installations that may endanger the civilian population, such as those directed at dams, dikes and nuclear plants.

International humanitarian law exists above all to protect human beings, to alleviate or, where possible, prevent their suffering. It is applicable to all armed conflicts – international or national – whatever their cause. But the scope of international humanitarian law is wider still, since it also seeks to preserve human dignity by means of the humanitarian aid it provides. The four Geneva Conventions of 1949 and their two Additional Protocols unequivocally affirm the right of the victims of conflict to assistance and protection. The law specifies that impartial relief work must not be regarded either as interference in an armed conflict or as a hostile act, even if the aid is intended for civilians supporting the enemy. It includes special provisions requiring the parties to the conflict to grant free passage to relief consignments. Although assistance and access to the victims does impinge upon the sovereignty of the states concerned, such an action today has a basis in law.

Humanitarian law is complementary to human rights law, both being concerned with respect for the individual and individual fundamental rights, such as the right to life. Human rights law assigns governments a responsibility towards their own nationals and gives citizens certain rights *vis-à-vis* their own governments, while humanitarian law concentrates on the situation of an individual who is subject – potentially or in fact – to arbitrary action by the enemy, be that enemy foreign or of the same nationality, whether a government or an armed opposition group. But the fact that this law applies to them as well does not constitute international recognition of armed groups. The present system of protection may seem complex, especially in the case of internal strife, where only human rights are applicable and protection is thus weakened.

Where the implementation of international humanitarian law is concerned, the ICRC has a special role not only in promoting the law but also as a neutral intermediary during armed conflicts. While maintaining contact among the warring parties with a view to solving problems of humanitarian concern, it also serves as an intermediary between the victims of conflict – who enjoy certain rights – and the states having obligations towards them.

From the legal point of view, there is a gap between the situation within the state – where police forces and courts can help citizens to enforce their rights – and the international stage, on which there is neither court nor police force having authority over the parties to a conflict. The victims' fate thus too often depends on the goodwill of the parties concerned.

Compliance with international humanitarian law is ultimately ensured by the rule contained in Article 1 common to the four Geneva Conventions obliging the states party to those instruments to 'respect and ensure respect for the present Convention in all circumstances'. Although this obligation mainly concerns states that are themselves involved in a conflict, all the states thereby become responsible should a warring state, including a state itself party to the Conventions, violate the law. To meet this obligation, they can not only take bilateral measures but also call on the United Nations – invoking its Charter – or other (regional) organisations to take appropriate action.

With regard to the repression of war crimes, genocide and crimes against humanity, current efforts to establish an international criminal court are most welcome. The International Fact-Finding Commission, provided for in Article 90 of Protocol I, and international tribunals such as those set up for the former Yugoslavia and Rwanda are all bodies that implement humanitarian law. These trends, although still tentative, are worthy of support.

International humanitarian law has been developed considerably in recent years, but the implementation of that law is by no means satisfactory. The ICRC and other organisations that have witnessed all too frequent violations of the law in armed conflicts have no other course of action than to call upon the states and armed groups concerned to respect this law. The states bound by the law, however, show very little inclination to take action.

◆◆◆

41 ◆ Neutrality and Impartiality: Fundamental Rights
Carlo von Flüe

The principle of neutrality

Neutrality obviously means that you support neither one side nor the other. The ultimate objective here, however, is not neutrality itself. As a tool in humanitarian endeavour, neutrality is a way of facilitating impartial action, action devoid of discrimination.

While it is neutral as regards ideology and the interests of the opposing sides in conflict, the ICRC is not 'neutral' when it comes to helping the victims of the fighting and all those not or no longer taking part in the hostilities. On the contrary, it actively defends their interests. In order to promote the interests of the wounded, the sick and prisoners – whether civilian or military – and to act on behalf of the civilian population, the ICRC must have direct and regular access to those victims.

Though we insist that humanitarian work must be neutral, this is not to deny the impact of that work on frequently unstable political and military relationships. But the authorities, if they are still in power, remain responsible for the survival of their fellow citizens. They have no right to exploit international aid as a means of freeing themselves from their obligations, and so use for their own purposes resources meant to honour those obligations.

Some organisations prefer the term 'non-partisan action' to the word 'neutrality'. This was the case for those who adopted the Code of Conduct for the International Red Cross and Red Crescent Movement and non-governmental organisations in disaster relief. An outside humanitarian agency must not take sides in a conflict. This does not mean that it cannot protest in the event of a flagrant violation of humanitarian law, but it should be clear about how it does this, and adept at using a whole range of possibilities from open condemnation to discreet diplomatic approaches.

The ICRC's neutrality is often wrongly equated with the confidentiality it practises in conducting some of its activities. Confidentiality is simply a working method, not a principle. It would create difficulties indeed if an ICRC delegate, leaving a place of detention, were to condemn publicly the ill-treatment that he had found there, for in all likelihood the organisation would never be allowed to return, and the detainees might be subjected to further treatment of the same kind – if not worse.

The principle of impartiality

In the face of human suffering, no distinction may be made with respect to nationality, race, religion, social position, political affiliation or any other similar criterion. Any distinction between persons eligible for humanitarian assistance is unacceptable. Nationals of the country that is the victim of aggression and nationals of the aggressor all have the same right to protection and assistance, even if the 'politically correct' international attitude is that the former are the 'good victims'.

In such a situation, working for the least privileged and most vulnerable population groups does not mean flouting the principle of impartiality, for real impartiality lies in helping individuals according only to their need, giving priority to those in the most urgent distress. Like all principles, that of impartiality is open to criticism, but without the approach it prescribes, the confidence of the various parties will inevitably be lost forever.

Willing as it is to open its field of endeavour to others, the ICRC sees an ever-growing number of organisations with at best vaguely defined responsibilities and mandates entering its sphere of action: United Nations agencies, representatives of regional organisations, peace-keeping forces and non-governmental organisations. What is remark-able is that most of them claim to be following the same principles of humanity, impartiality and neutrality. Yet all run the same risk: the sub-merging of humanitarian work in a political process, and thus ulti-mately being politicised themselves. It should never be forgotten that humanitarian action needs to be dissociated from any effort to resolve a conflict. The two may certainly be complementary, but they must always remain clearly separate.

◆◆◆

42 ◆ Neutrality and Impartiality
JUDY EL BUSHRA

What is the practical significance of the concept of impartiality, in the context of real situations in the field? ACORD's experience in imple-menting development operations in emergency contexts is noteworthy from this point of view. Indeed, all the African countries in which the agency operates have been affected by armed conflicts in the past years.

ACORD has drawn some strong convictions from this experience. It has learned that distinguishing between emergency, rehabilitation and development does not help in facing the real problem of providing short-term aid within the framework of long-term objectives. And it has concluded that it is fallacious to think that humanitarian agencies can, or should, remain neutral during conflict situations. Through their presence in the field and their central position in controlling certain key resources, NGOs are inevitably and actively implicated in conflicts. Moreover, in certain situations they may deem it necessary to take sides – such as, for instance, when we are convinced that the best way to serve the poor is to oppose the individuals or factions behind corrup-tion and injustice. In the Rwandan crisis, for example, it seemed impossible to support the call for a ceasefire because, as far as we were concerned, the advance by the Rwandan Popular Forces (RPF) repre-sented the best hope of ending the massacres.

Guided by these convictions, ACORD endeavours to support certain fundamental principles such as justice and equality and apply them coherently. Adopting a strategy of impartiality allows it to reinforce persons, actions or trends that potentially could lead to a decrease in hostilities.

So much for theory. In reality, the contradictions, complexities and moral dilemmas remain. In this respect, impartiality is scarcely of greater use than neutrality. To make the concept of impartiality more relevant at the operational level, we must examine its concrete manifestations. Four areas of analysis must be considered: (1) the agency staff member as an individual; (2) the programme team; (3) the operational policy of the organisation; and (4) the position of the organisation with respect to the other actors on the international scene.

From the point of view of the staff member as an individual, the most serious dilemma is whether or not to bear witness to the human rights abuses one has observed in carrying out one's duties. Speaking out could endanger the humanitarian worker. Moreover, in a polarised political context, this testimony could be interpreted as partisan and could compromise the rest of the action. For example, certain members of ACORD's staff in Rwanda believe that they cannot advocate forgiveness and reconciliation in their work if they do not at the same time denounce the atrocities committed by certain members of the communities in which they are working.

Programme teams are confronted by the same dilemmas as the staff members. If programmes are to have an influence on the resolution of a conflict at the local level, they must have the trust of all sectors of the community, which implies developing relations with all the parties present, even if this entails compromise. In Chad, for example, ACORD endeavoured, at the local level, to encourage the military to produce official, written requests each time they requisitioned our vehicles – rather than simply demanding that the vehicles be turned over to them. This helped to promote a minimum level of mutual respect and to protect our staff. It is easy to take an uncompromising stand when one is defining policy guidelines in London or Paris, but it is more difficult when faced with an armed, inebriated individual.

The composition of the teams is another important issue. From ACORD's point of view, balanced representation – reflecting the composition of the community – presents a relative guarantee of impartiality. If one believes that solidarity is possible among opposing groups, then this belief should be demonstrated in the comportment of the team members. The ACORD teams in Mali and Somalia have proved that this solidarity exists, and this is one of the reasons why ACORD has not withdrawn from these countries.

It is not reasonable, however, to expect members of the staff (or the partner organisations) to be unaffected by the events that take place in the community in which they live. Differences of opinion and mistrust among members of the staff can endanger certain individuals and create power struggles for the control of funding, information and other project-related resources. As a result, the agency could be seriously compromised in the eyes of the community as a whole.

Regarding *operational policy*, great care is required to ensure that our presence in an area is not exploited for propaganda purposes by one party or the other. We are afraid that in some cases our presence conferred a veneer of legitimacy on the oppressors. Even more seriously, it can help fuel the conflict by bringing in hard currency (salaries, hiring of security guards) and because its resources may be hijacked to support armed groups. In this way, the agencies provide support to the predators who perpetuate the conflict.

The ability of the agency to identify the differences within communities and to target those groups that are particularly vulnerable is another important aspect of impartiality. Recognising this vulnerability requires complex, informed analysis. Without it, there is a danger that aid will end up in the hands of those who already have the power.

Finally, whether they like it or not, *NGOs are part of the international economic order* that determines the political and military priorities of our governments (as demonstrated in Bosnia), influences the information that is spread by the media and conditions the demands of the donors. This form of pressure can lead to ill-conceived, ill-timed intervention.

Four suggestions to lower the risks and promote guidelines for action

First, it is crucial that NGOs accept that their role is a political one, that the actions they undertake are not neutral and have an impact on people's lives: accordingly, they must base their actions on political analysis.

Second, NGOs must ensure that the relations they establish with grassroots communities are based on solid foundations that respect the integrity of all the partners. This does not mean unconditional acceptance of the others' ideas, but enables the destitute and the excluded – our partners of choice – to take over our projects for themselves on an equal footing. Finally, this is the only guarantee of security for ACORD and its staff.

Third, we must invest a great deal more than we do at present in local programme teams, especially as concerns training, reinforcing team spirit and management. This training should cover areas that until now were never considered as belonging to the field of development, such as human rights training. The status of the staff must also be defined in order to clarify their rights and duties in conflict situations.

Fourth, we must establish networks to reinforce lobbying by creating alliances between countries and between organisations to ensure that the debate on impartiality and the role of NGOs is based on accurate information and analysis. An important guarantee of impartiality, at the local and international levels, is the establishment of organisational links between field programmes and the advocacy organisations that complement them.

◆◆◆

43 ◆ The Rwandan Crisis: Impartiality, Reconcialition and Justice
ACORD

The Rwandan crisis in 1994 highlighted the dilemma surrounding neutrality. At the time, ACORD had two programmes inside the country and one in Kigali. All three were wiped out by the events in April of that year and, for several weeks, ACORD concentrated its efforts on tracing its staff.

When an emergency programme was launched in early May in the north of Rwanda, ACORD found itself in the zone controlled by the RPF. There were several practical reasons for this. ACORD had already worked in this region and logistical support was available through existing programmes in Uganda. Without any base in Burundi or in Zaïre, it was difficult for ACORD to gain access to government-controlled areas. The area controlled by the RPF, unlike the government-controlled areas, offered at least minimal security guarantees. However, ACORD was determined to work in the government-controlled areas if at all possible. ACORD's decision was sharply criticised. The organisation was accused of sympathising with the RPF and of renouncing the principle of neutrality. In the eyes of the other organisations, if a humanitarian group could work with only one party to the conflict, there should be no collaboration of any kind with any of the parties involved.

The position of ACORD was further complicated by its assessment of the situation, which differed from that of other organisations. It soon came to the conclusion that there were two conflicts:

♦ a civil war between the RPF and the Rwandan army;
♦ a campaign of massacres orchestrated by Hutu extremist parties, which clearly represented the greatest threat to the Rwandan population.

The international community being powerless to act, the RPF represented the best hope of ending the massacres. Therefore, ACORD did not support the call for a ceasefire between the RPF and the army under the auspices of the UN, as this would have consolidated the front line and allowed the massacres to continue behind it.

ACORD was not neutral with regard to the two parties involved, although its position remained impartial and based on its mandate, and the agency had no political allegiance to any of the parties. Its fundamental objective remained that of working with the poor of Rwanda — the farming community, which was predominantly Hutu — even if being considered a partisan of the RPF could prevent ACORD from accomplishing its mission.

Nevertheless, it is the duty of development NGOs to work for reconciliation through actions at the grassroots level. They should leave it to the human rights organisations to rule on past responsibility for atrocities.

44 • Dealing with Inconsistencies
YANNICK LASSICA

Before the crisis

Before the crisis set off by the *coup d'état* on 21 October 1993, Burundi sustained a delicate balance between important assets that contributed to a strong economic, social and cultural fabric, and negative elements that generated a certain structural violence, sowing the seeds for future crisis.

The build-up

The authorities have always acted to minimise the crisis, while maintaining a façade of normality for casual observers.

Most of the many local development initiatives we observed were survival activities. Others were merely smokescreens for belligerent, or simply criminal, organisations.

The instability of interlocutors within the administration was accentuated by the power struggles between factions, with the result that decisions that had been negotiated previously were regularly nullified.

Since 21 October 1993, radical Tutsi circles have been trying to take over the workings of the state, of the administration, and of society. Thus Bujumbura, which was the official capital, is now a controlled city.

Information, which was already crucial in peacetime, has become an essential strategic element of the conflict.

Parameters of the crisis

This crisis is simultaneously cyclothymic and itinerant. It peaks locally, reaching paroxysms of barbarity that leave no one unscathed. Fear has gradually become visceral and now affects everyone. Perceived and real insecurity as well as physical violence compel everyone to function within his or her own safety perimeter, which changes from day to day.

The social fabric and relations between individuals are disintegrating and changing gradually. Locally, this phenomenon is accompanied by a social reshuffle. Within its own sphere of lawlessness the crisis is generating its own war economy.

Changes which disrupt the decision-making process

The parameters of the crisis directly affect the functioning of the networks

134

and sources of information and knowledge of all the field operators. They influence individuals in the cooperation organisations. This results in a mal-functioning of the decision-making process: crisis can be understood as a broad and profound inequality of chances in life and in the face of corrup-tion, of the arbitrary, of impunity, and of a lack of access to information, education, health and basic necessities. The state and the aid system are omnipresent, authoritarian and condescending, limiting rather than amelior-ating the prospects of most of the people.

Inadequate analysis, follow-up, and monitoring

In crisis situations, the ability of the actors to carry out global, relevant and up-to-date analysis, the indispensable prerequisite for any decision or prognosis, is affected to a certain degree. Some cooperation organisations neglect to undertake a complete, relevant investigation of the situation or a serious socio-political analysis. The organisations' findings may also be distorted by the 'ivory tower' syndrome if their executives, whether posted in the crisis-ridden country on long or short missions, work almost exclu-sively in the capital where they are isolated from the realities of the rest of the country, yet feel confident to make decisions on the overall situation.

Misinterpretation in the decision-making process

Crisis, a lawless environment, is favourable to individuals and cooperation organisations that are not very particular about the meaning of their action:

- Convenience and the interests of individuals or institutions supersede the public interest. 'Cushy' niches and empty partnerships proliferate.
- The staff of the cooperation organisations take sides in the conflict.
- Organisations make decisions contrary to their own ethics and those they wish to impose on others.

Decisions must be ethical and professional

The first proposal: The decision to intervene in a country in conflict should be structured.

- One must have the capacity to intervene in a complex situation, based on an experience both of conflict situations and of the same country in peacetime.
- One must work closely with local and international networks to develop a source of relevant information and knowledge.
- One must structure the meaning of the intervention on the basis of clear ethical principles.
- One must negotiate and test one's legitimacy.

The second proposal: Thorough and systematic self-examination is necessary before taking action. It is essential to be able to justify one's objectives, one's choice of partners, area of intervention, programme of action, methods, diagnosis, and follow-up monitoring capability, one's attitude in the field, and one's way of dealing with security and human rights issues.

The third proposal: Even in peacetime, one must take into account the potential for future crisis involving structural violence, disregard for human rights and power-related factors. These realities should reflect in one's approach, diagnosis, follow-up monitoring system and decision-making process.

The lawlessness, violence and insecurity that prevail in a country in conflict are fertile terrain for inconsistencies. At some point in its history and to some degree, every cooperation organisation is prone to the inconsistencies and malfunctioning in the decision-making process described here. This means that professionals and their organisations must be particularly vigilant during crises. The capitalisation and exchange that are occurring through growing international experience in the fields of development and emergency should help to contain inconsistencies in the future.

IV. iii

Relations of NGOs with Public Authorities and Guerrilla Movements during Transition Phases

The relations that NGOs enjoy with the public authorities of the countries in which they intervene or with the organisations that oppose them (or opposed them in the recent past) form a contrasted body which echoes the community to which they belong.

Several approaches emerge:

◆ Some NGOs do not wish to maintain steady relations with the governments of the countries they assist, justifying this position by claiming that to be non-governmental is to work exclusively with civilian populations. They are content to rely on functional relations with the public authorities to be able to intervene on the basis of a mandate that they alone have defined.

◆ Others have undertaken an in-depth examination of relations with public authorities or their opponents, and whether or not it is necessary to maintain these relations during conflicts.

◆ Among NGOs, a third trend is that the actions they implement are part of the dynamics of the social organisations that are evolving during crises.

◆◆◆

45 ◆ Relations with Public Authorities in Afghanistan
PHILIPPE TRUZE

Some have characterised the ongoing conflict in Afghanistan in terms of the relationship of its society with its government. In a first stage, Afghan society was opposed to the government (resistance to the

Communist regime and its Soviet allies); in a second stage, society was without governance (establishment of self-administered free zones and a co-presence of the government and the occupying power); finally, the present stage, society in search of a government.

In Afghanistan as elsewhere the problem of rebuilding the state is not limited to restoring public authorities or a national administration. Rebuilding a national identity and a diversified political body that plays by at least some of the rules of democracy, healing the wounds, and other important steps in the process of national reconstruction are not on the agenda of most NGOs.[2] On the other hand, the activities the latter conduct are not neutral when it comes to rebuilding a national or multi-regional administration. Afghanistan is an eloquent illustration of these relations, all the more so as in certain regions of the country emergency, development and rehabilitation situations are interlinked. Every operator is compelled to become involved in these diverse activities. We will not at this point go into the issue of line-crossing between the territories held by various factions; it can be summed up as a matter of familiarity with the conflicting parties and of the astuteness of local logisticians.

A conflict never totally eradicates an administration

An administration is a functional, or potentially functional, body of structures and facilities, technical and administrative procedures, and personnel who enjoy a legitimacy conferred on them by the recognition of at least a significant portion of the population and work towards a specific objective (technical, for example).

According to the above definition, it can be affirmed that in many conflict situations fragments of local, regional and/or central administrations subsist here and there. To find them one must want to look for them. To look for them, one must have an interest in finding them. This explains why, in many situations, certain major organisations that have no interest in strengthening local technical administrations claim that they do not exist.

Our experience of Afghanistan leads us to believe that, in the emergency phase, seeking out these fragments of administrations to establish operational partnerships with them is not only effective for implementing low-cost emergency activities, but constitutes a decisive contribution to the subsequent reconstruction of relations between the public authorities and the population. How can such fragments, be they large or small, survive very harsh political/ military conflicts?

Men (and women)

In the first place, the *esprit de corps* of an administration which in many ways quite closely resembles the French administration, subsists, and even endures, remarkable for the permanence of its mid-level manage-. ment, in spite of constantly changing governments and regimes. The ministers come and go, die even, but the directors remain. We were surprised to find in the Ministry of Health in Kabul several civil servants we had known twenty years earlier, before the Communists came to power. In 1996, 50 to 75 per cent of the technical cadres of the Ministry had already been in place during the Communist regime, while six or seven ministers had succeeded one another in the Ministry of Health since the fall of the Communists in April 1992. The advent of the Taliban, considered the most radical masters of the city, has borne out this observation. Civil servants tend to survive the most adverse conditions, even when a state is totally bankrupt or devotes all its funds to the war effort and can no longer pay them (in Kabul, they are still receiving the cash portion of their remuneration, which is negligible, whereas the compensation they used to receive in the form of staple foods and basic necessities has vanished altogether). In the capital, the civil servants continue to check in at the ministries every week and even stay for a few hours. The reasons for this dedication must be examined in detail but one might hypothesise that they do not want to prejudice their future, but wish to remain on the registers so as not to lose their entitlements, particularly their pension (the government sometimes gives land in lieu of cash) in hope of a better tomorrow. This weekly appointment has proved very important because the informa-tion of interest to civil servants circulates in this manner; when an NGO, AVICEN, informed the Ministry that some activities could be conducted jointly with administrative personnel and technicians from the Ministry of Health, the people in question (such as doctors from the centres for mother and child care, or vaccination technicians) re-appeared as if by magic, although foreign humanitarian aid actors had claimed that the ministries no longer had any operational capacity.

Premises, buildings and equipment

The presence of civil servants is the main thing. Buildings, in wartime, are incidental. We saw ministries (or fragments of administrations) organised in makeshift premises, moving about town to avoid the shelling. Only certain specific activities require purpose-built struc-tures (surgery for example), and then not always.

As for equipment, we were amazed to witness the reappearance, intact, from cellars and hiding places of material and equipment that had been carefully stowed away out of harm's reach and brought out again when it could be put to good use. Certain civil servants even seemed to consider themselves personally responsible for the equipment necessary for their work (such as the refrigerators of the vaccination technicians).

Procedures

As for an administrative vacuum, there is no such thing. There remains always a time-honoured procedure upon which a fragment of an administration can fall back to justify its actions, or pseudo-actions (at this stage efficiency is not a criterion). The foreigner is sometimes surprised by such procedures, instituted by a previous regime politically scorned by the current one, and that no one feels compromised by their – not always neutral – resurgence. Then again, most often the previous regime will have drawn heavily on its predecessor for inspiration so that, in the end, administrative procedures acquire a temporal inertia which holds them in place by default.

Real versus virtual administration

A majority of personnel in attendance in offices and clinics versus one that can be easily mobilised; administrative premises in their original buildings versus makeshift offices scattered about the town; a state that does or does not pay salaries and provide adequate budgetary means: these are the differences between an existing administrative fragment and a potentially existing one, a sort of virtual administrative fragment that could become real if the will and the essential ingredients to revive it existed.

The ingredients for reactivating an administration

We should first point out that the objective is rarely to reactivate an entire ministry but rather only one of its departments, such as mother and child care (MCC), hospital administration or vaccination. Generally, and this is no coincidence, the department that interests specialised emergency NGOs is one that corresponds more or less to one of the previously described administrative fragments. As a matter of affinity, vaccinators tend to congregate with other vaccinators, prevention specialists with other prevention specialists, surgeons with surgeons, and so on.

Thus, in Kabul, the entire MCC department had remained more or less well-knit, in reality or potentially. Once the NGO made it known to the Ministry and its civil servants that it had obtained the means to set up an MCC emergency system based on the former MCC system of the ministry, things went very fast. The financial incentive to be paid to the staff was decided in agreement with the Ministry, thus supplementing their basic salary to arrive at a decent level of remuneration (although still inferior to that paid by NGOs to their own local staff). Procedures were established for the procurement of equipment and supplies (medicines, vaccines, nutritional supplements and so on) by the NGO, as were the respective areas of responsibility for the management of stocks and distribution. It was decided what adjustments were necessary to technical procedures and often obsolete methods harking back to a distant past (in Afghanistan, these procedures dated back to before the treaty of Alma Ata). Finally, the contribution of the Ministry was determined. Mostly in kind, it would nevertheless considerably lighten the budget of the NGO (free premises, rehabilitated vehicles and equipment, heating, a portion of the salaries, customs waivers).

The advantages

The first immediate advantage is the ability to act quickly at a significant level in response to a vital problem. Where a traditional NGO can set up one to three MCC emergency structures, partnership with an administration permits the reactivating of ten to twenty for an equivalent outlay of effort, time and money.

The second advantage in the longer term, is to ensure the survival of the administration by employing its personnel, equipment and structures. This prevents the classical scenario of brain drain towards the NGOs, which offer higher salaries. Through the transmission of certain techniques and modern methods the administration regains credibility vis-à-vis the NGOs, the donors and the specialised UN agencies. It acquires a technical legitimacy it was lacking that puts it in good posture for the rehabilitation phase. This is indeed what happened in the MCC department in Kabul, where the centres that had been reactivated thanks to emergency funding survived after the funding was stopped. The United Nations can now work more easily with the Ministry and a certain number of other NGOs have followed the example of the pioneering NGO.

The disadvantages

This approach requires a real understanding of the local actors and current politics, together with the experience to be able to determine the degree of passivity and permanence of the administration. It is therefore not accessible to traditional NGOs which rely on a rapid turnover of young, inexperienced staff who have little knowledge of the subtleties involved in relations with public authorities. These NGOs tend to offer expensive, unsustainable, ready-made solutions.

Another disadvantage is that this type of initiative can be slow to get off the ground. Things speed up once everyone in the administration has measured the advantages offered by new techniques and methods, and by a partnership with a specialised NGO. A certain amount of time is needed to optimise the benefit for the administration (legitimacy) and for the NGO (technical capacity).

But the major inconvenience is posed by traditional NGOs and by the executives of funding structures who feel, rightly perhaps, that their relevance is challenged, their own approach being, in contrast, heavy, costly and fragile. NGOs that promote the institutional approach can be subjected to all sorts of manoeuvring, generally targeting the minor shortcomings inherent in collaboration with an institution and which usually disappear over time.

Relations between the central administration and peripheral (provincial, regional) administrations

In spite of political or even military division of the national territory, local administrations generally try to preserve sector-based technical relations with their capitals. Thus, the provincial administrator of the MCC programme keeps in touch with his counterpart in the Ministry, first to continue to receive the small subsidies the central administration will keep on sending in an attempt to maintain a semblance of control over the situation in the provinces, but also because everyone is looking towards the future. Everyone knows that peace will return the Ministry and the central administration to the privileged position of sole interlocutor of the international donors.

Compatibility with the societal approach

The institutional approach does not prevent an NGO from conducting a simultaneous societal, community-based approach in the neighbourhoods and villages. On the contrary, this dual approach gives a clear idea of the financial and political responsibilities that should devolve to the communities in the future. It affords an early understanding of the dynamics on which civil society will be rebuilt.

◆◆◆

46 ◆ Peru: Working in Areas Controlled by the Shining Path
JEAN-JACQUES BOUTROU

The coexistence in the same area of a guerrilla movement like the Shining Path (SP) and teams working for development is contradictory. The former demands compliance with its *diktat* and violent hegemonism (the imposition of a model, elimination of undesirable individuals), whereas the action of the latter rests on humanistic values that have been integrated by the population. On 3 December 1988 the murder of three project team members from the Centre international de coopération pour le développement agricole (CICDA) project team caused many NGOs to withdraw from rural or suburban areas where the SP is present. But commitments had been made to the population: isolated and caught in the crossfire between the SP and the army, they requested that links and actions be maintained.

How to take action without endangering the leaders of the farming communities, the development agents, the local elected representatives whose values are so different from those of the SP? The perseverance of many NGOs brought about the creation of remote-control support systems with only occasional follow-up visits to the field. These partnerships were characterised by discretion and the absence of on-the-spot project structures, permanent staff or logistical capacity, to avoid becoming an easy target. The system of cooperation reorganised in early 1989 was based on structures already in place or emerging, each pursuing portions of projects or simply preserving what had been achieved thus far with a view to redeployment once favourable conditions were restored.

For example, in Chumbivilcas actions continued to be carried out through a group of 45 affiliated farming communities. This organisation became the motor for local development by organising activities for marketing, processing of agricultural produce, and technical and financial services. A small team furnished by CICDA and based in Lima provided methodological, logistical and administrative support. In Haquira (population 10,000) the municipality took over the activities. In the province of Espinar the relay was ensured by a local NGO created by former local employees of CICDA.

These examples show that a variety of systems exist in conflict situations but all take into account first and foremost the plans and safety of the actors. The struggle for development does not concern only living conditions, food and health; it also concerns values. Can one renounce these values and conduct activities that support a model which does not correspond to the aspiration of the population and is contrary to the most elementary principles of human rights?

The approach of all development NGOs must be based on the identification and recognition of local dynamics and on respect for the population's aspirations. The guerrilla movement imposed its own analyses and model of social and economic structuring, however, disregarding the aspirations of the population. The forcible enrolment of men into the ranks of the guerrillas to massacre civilians in other areas is not only contrary to the fundamental values of respect for life that CICDA shared with the Quechua population; it also totally opposes the process of local development.

47 ◆ Contributing to the Management of a Transition Period between Conflicts and Prospects of Decentralisation in North Mali
ANDRÉ MARTY

On 11 April 1992 the signing of the national pact – between the Azawad (Tuareg and Arab) movements and unified fronts, and the Government of Mali – created in principle the conditions for a balanced settlement and the return to a peace that had been disrupted by two consecutive years of murderous unrest, emigration and economic asphyxia. It was within this framework that the young institution Commissariat au Nord organised a mission composed of IRAM consultants and national executives to define the modalities for the resumption of activities in the northern part of the country.

It was clear from the start that the situation in the north was very complex. A vicious circle was created by enduring insecurity, on the one hand, and on the other the need to conduct actions that would encompass emergency, development and the rehabilitation of projects, infrastructures and institutional parameters, as the state no longer had any real representation at the district level (the bottom rung of the general administration). Concretely, this represented three closely linked and challenging problems that had to be treated jointly:

- How to achieve lasting peace, security and reconciliation where the social fabric has been destroyed?
- How to reinstate the state in a manner which inspires trust?
- How to encourage economic recovery?

In answer to these questions, several proposals were drawn up and put into practice in 1993.

1. Mobile support teams (MST)[3] for peace and the planned development process were created for each of the three regions (Timbuktu, Gao and Kidal). These teams were to be as representative as possible of the diverse local populations and would fulfil three functions which follow from the problems defined above:

   - working for peace and social reconciliation;
   - facilitating the return of the administration in a manner that would involve local representatives (by setting up and supporting District Transition Assemblies – DTAs);
   - accelerating the emergency–rehabilitation–development process.

2. A DTA was created for each district. This is a new type of structure bringing together the head of the district, who presides, and local representatives who reflect the diversity of the population so that no group feels excluded. The latter were to be designated by local consensus. Once set up, the DTA was to exercise collective responsibility for the management of local affairs. As its name implies, this institution was conceived as a temporary structure for each of the three northern regions. It would disappear once the districts were replaced by municipalities throughout the country, which was to take place shortly. But in the meanwhile these bodies were a means of experimenting in local management and preparing for future decentralisation.

145

3. The development committees that existed at the level of the regional and local seats, comprised mainly of state agents, were extended to members of civil society (development projects, NGOs, deputies and representatives of the political parties, resource persons) to enable the principal driving forces to collaborate effectively in seeking appropriate solutions.

4. Development projects were redefined to take into account changes linked to the constitution of the third Republic and the democratic institutions, to the signing of the National Pact and to the ground-work for decentralisation.

This plan very rapidly proved effective. While working actively to create the DTAs, the MSTs soon acquired a keen understanding of local realities. Thanks to their composition (each had four members of different social origins), their teamwork, and the trust they enjoyed in the various milieus, they were able to complete their mission. Their performance soon drew the attention of north-bound missions and delegations. The latter increasingly requested that they accompany them, with the result that their programmes with the DTA were some-times disrupted by these unexpected requests. Moreover, they partici-pated in the national deliberations conducted by the Decentralisation Mission charged with the creation of the future municipalities through-out Mali.

This original experiment has taught us a great deal. In the context of post-National Pact Mali – when government bodies (administrative and technical) were struggling to assert a presence in the field, but when insecurity, although quite real, appeared to be residual – setting up temporary facilities proved to be possible. Their role was to recreate the conditions for dialogue within the population, and between it and the administrators. To do this, MSTs and DTAs had to turn their efforts towards several areas:

◆ they had to take into account security and social reconciliation problems, in particular by supporting the inter-community encoun-ters which would proliferate after the escalation of tensions in 1994;

◆ they had to step up the recovery of economic activity (markets, mobility of individuals, merchandise and livestock, supply) in the perspective of the emergency–rehabilitation–development continuum (reviving – or even creating – new projects);

◆ they had to manage local affairs by compromising between the old type of administration that had no connection to the government and the new, experimental decentralised administration.

With the first communal elections coming up and with the DTAs and MSTs on the point of making way for the new structures as planned, the experience of these transitional institutions has taught us many lessons for the future, not only for North Mali itself, but perhaps also for other contexts.

◆◆◆

48 ◆ Building New Dynamics: the Example of North Mali
BERNARD HUSSON

The recent armed conflict in North Mali was not the first. This region has been hit by a number of disasters in the past 25 years (see André Marty, Part II, Chapter 11, pages 39–40). This one, however, was resolved without the intervention of an international military force and, consequently, without arousing the financial interest of the international community at the time of the return to peace.

The prevailing situation in North Mali underscores the complexity of the approaches to be developed in a post-conflict environment:

◆ Must one work in the same way with the groups engaged in the conflict as with those who did not take part? Must actions address the needs of the entire population or should they be aimed primarily at those groups that are most vulnerable (returnees)?

◆ How can one involve the local authorities who represent the central government that was favourable to the peace process but also a party to the conflict?

◆ How does one make the transition from free public services during the conflict (in the refugee camps in Mauritania, in the facilities that continued to function in Mali) to partial cost-recovery without the return to peace being associated with increased economic hardship?

◆ How does one adjust the conflict zone to the changes that occurred in the rest of the country, including the decentralisation and establishment of municipalities, and the privatisation of public services such as health?

Lessons learned

1. As soon as tension abates and especially if a cessation of hostilities has been signed, one must work with legal local institutions to reinforce their legitimacy. It is advisable to facilitate the reinstatement of the administration and consequently to arrange for a minimum of facilities and lodgings for its civil servants. An additional difficulty, and not a minor one, is that the integrity of the civil servants in place must be scrutinised to avoid unlawful practices that could cause tensions in areas that remain unstable.

2. Simultaneously, the potential leaders of the decentralised municipalities being formed must be trained to identify priority needs, as all facilities do not have the same level of priority. In North Mali, the rehabilitation of water installations was the first priority, followed by schools, health facilities and administrative buildings. This stage of the action also aims to reassess areas of complementarity between the different groups (breeders of livestock, farmers, tradespeople and others) that are the basis of a return to normal.

3. Rather than seeking to introduce definitive modes of institutional functioning as soon as the conflict is over, one must build an evolutionary capacity. For instance, it would be illusory to envisage, at an early stage, that the population would participate financially in the upkeep of infrastructures. One way of dealing with the difficult transition from free aid to financial participation could be to open a debate well ahead of time on the population's ability to take over running costs.

4. Activities of an economic nature must be supported early on to avoid a climate of dependence.

5. Plans of action should not be drawn up for refugees only, but should be open to all (this is borne out by observations made in other countries).

6. The deterioration of infrastructures, of economic activity and of the environment[4] raises the awareness of the population of the need for outside assistance. People know that national resources alone cannot stimulate local growth. Consequently, external assistance is

well received (although care must be taken not to present it as a panacea).

A role for external operators

1. The stabilisation of the situation does not follow a linear path, and support must take into account a constantly evolving context: periods of progress, of inactivity or even of renewed tension.

2. The precarious living conditions of the population should not lead to the assumption that it has a common vision of the future. On the contrary, diversity is the rule in the rate of organisation of the different groups; in their resources; and in their agendas and priorities. These constraints can be turned into opportunities for debate on organisation and the relations between groups, making it essential to strengthen the role of mediation and at the same time that of the operator. Responding to the demands of the population is therefore an incentive to work with each group separately at first before widening the scope of activities.

3. Confusion must be avoided. Once the acute emergency phase is over, there is a proliferation of all sorts of interventions. At that point, the risk arises that these actions may be inconsistent,[5] especially as insufficient administrative and technical personnel cannot ensure their coherence. Should actors from outside the area unilaterally ensure coherence among themselves while being careful to avoid appearing as an opposition force?

◆◆◆

IV. iv

49 ◆ Relations between Humanitarians and the Military
Philippe Truze

Relations between humanitarians and the military cannot be dealt with globally. On the contrary, their analysis should take into account the contexts in which they occur. There are several types of situation

- The humanitarian interventions of a state are but one of the forms of action it can take to have a direct presence in the field, outside its borders.

- If there is a need for armed military protection of the operations conducted by humanitarian agencies, it is because the politico-military context and the way in which a humanitarian action is perceived by the population it benefits can present serious risks for the teams in the field.

- The rigour of military organisation can be very effective, particularly for health interventions requiring elaborate logistics. In this case, the issue of militarisation of emergency care is unavoidable.

Interventions of the state abroad and state humanitarian action

When a state is determined to defend its interests outside its borders, it opts for the form of intervention best suited to its means and to the importance of its interests. Technically, it must possess the necessary means for intervention; politically, it must be able to justify its action both in the area in which it intervenes (both to the parties to the conflict and to the population) and vis-à-vis the spectators (public opinion in its own and neighbouring countries). In any case, it must justify the planned or implemented action.

Thus, in France, outside actions are justified as being in defence of national strategic and/or economic interests; the duty to protect French nationals at risk; the moral duty to react to blatant violations of human rights; or in the name of the right (and duty) to interfere when local authorities can no longer cope with acute humanitarian crisis situations.

The modalities of intervention depend specifically on the balance of power and the historical relations between the intervening country and the host country and, more generally, on the world balance of power as it affects the interplay of alliances and spheres of influence. Consequently, the intervening country will use a variety of methods: armed intervention, economic and financial intervention, or humanitarian intervention.

If the balance of power is very unfavourable the intervention will be humanitarian only. But the humanitarian component can also be part of firmer and more direct intervention. It can occasionally even be a preliminary step or a cover. State humanitarian intervention is, in fact, rarely conducted separately from other military or economic action. When it is, it is an avowal of weakness in the balance of power between the 'interfering' state and that in which it interferes, the 'beneficiary' state. Today, the risk of deviation in state humanitarian action is real, because emergency medical, food, logistical and sanitation aid are justifiable in the name of the right (and duty) to interfere – a concept invented by the French and made official by the United Nations.

It is therefore important to place state humanitarian action back in the general context of international relations. To recall this context is to stress the fact that state humanitarian action is unrelated to moral ideals. It also underscores the fact that, although the means of control (parliamentary or other) of state humanitarian action must certainly be improved, they at least exist – whereas private humanitarian action is conducted without any technical, ethical or political control.

Finally, state humanitarian action has a major advantage in the traditional field of emergency. Technically, and in the very short term, recourse to military or militarised medical, sanitation and/or logistical units is always more efficient than the action of any NGO, even if it is specialised or endowed with strong logistical means.

Military/armed protection of humanitarian operations

Why is there a need for armed protection – which dispels at once the pious vision of humanitarian aid founded exclusively on selfless moral values, on ideals of neutrality and impartiality? The first reason is that the actions of NGO staff working in a context of extreme violence cannot be truly neutral. If one were to draw a map of the conflicts in which there has been no European intervention one would see large white patches: the regions of Algeria that lie outside the control of the Algiers regime, for example, or certain regions of China. In those areas, no humanitarian intervention is conceivable without military protection.

The second reason has to do with the violence borne by civilian populations in modern conflicts. They are increasingly taken hostage by the protagonists of the conflicts. It is precisely at these threatened populations that humanitarian actions are aimed. In some cases, military intervention makes it possible to provide them with the minimum of security they need in order to survive.

Other reasons for the military protection of humanitarian interventions in conflict areas include the inexperience of NGO staff. Volunteers are often young, with no knowledge of conflict situations or of the cultural and political contexts in which they must intervene, and are therefore liable to make mistakes that can compromise their own safety. In Afghanistan, for instance, most of the tragic incidents that struck the humanitarian community were caused by the ill-judged behaviour of young humanitarians who had been plunged into a dangerous situation without adequate preparation.

Media pressure is also a cause of imprudent behaviour. It prompts emergency NGOs to neglect danger: they must arrive on the scene ever faster, be ever more visible. Media pressure spares no one, neither NGOs subsidised by the large intergovernmental emergency agencies, which rate actions solely by their visibility, nor the self-funded NGOs that rely on the presence and coverage of the media for their survival.

The military, a model of organisation for emergency operations

The temptation to apply civil defence methods to humanitarian action is an old one. It is inspired by the efficiency of civil defence, due in some measure to its rigorous organisation – often partly or totally military in style. France's two largest cities have entrusted their emergency relief to the armed forces – the army in Paris, the navy in Marseilles. The fire department, although civilian, is organised according to military methods and tradition – uniform, rank, discipline – but retains the right to go on strike. At the founding of Bioforce (a French training association), whose graduates still form the mainspring of (French) emergency organisations, the idea was to train the 'non-commissioned officers' of international action.

But is it possible to follow through on this logic, merging formal, efficient organisation with a military structure of which organisational skill is but one aspect? If the idea of emergency intervention is to be assimilated with that of rapid, substitutive relief, then indisputably the most technical phases can be entrusted to 'militarised' units, whether civilian or military. In the reality of the field, however, pure substitutive intervention – which would justify the use of predetermined technical procedures – is relatively rare. In all other cases, the infinite variety of situations that have been encountered renders the effectiveness of these procedures illusory, mortgaging the future of the beneficiary countries. The same argument suggests the advantage of the methodological approaches of which this work attempts to demonstrate the relevance and effectiveness.

The debate on this point could be modified by the cultural changes that are taking place in French society. Will the change to a professional army, together with the end of conscription, give rise to different forms of civil service – of which some might be designated for external humanitarian interventions?

Humanitarian aid – fact or fiction?

Faced with the dwindling number of armed protection missions carried out under the auspices of the United Nations in recent years, it is conceivable that alternative scenarios will be mounted. There are signs of change that will profoundly modify the humanitarian scene. Some of these signs are particularly ambiguous. Although the emergence of a new breed of humanitarian organisation, not necessarily Western or European but Asian or from the Gulf countries, is a favourable development, how can their approach to humanitarian intervention be articulated with that of the long-established organisations? Like the organisations that have sprung up recently in our hemisphere, they use humanitarian action as a propaganda tool, a means of religious expansionism, as an instrument of domination of the populations they 'assist'.

The first manifestations of this change that have been observed in Albania, for example, lead one to cast a new and watchful eye. Was the objective of the private militias raised by certain NGOs to protect the distribution of food aid, or did the food aid serve as a cover for arms transfers? The highly precise targeting of the beneficiaries of the aid seems to indicate a deviation which should be contained before it is too late. The experience of 150 years of history, confirmed by the scale of the actions conducted world-wide in the past 30 years, shows clearly that solidarity cannot be divided.

◆◆◆

153

50 ◆ What Role for the Military in Rehabilitation?
Véronique de Geoffroy

The emergence of state humanitarian aid, or rather its reappearance since the end of the Cold War, has resulted, in many Western countries and international organisations, in the concept of humanitarian diplomacy. The establishment of ECHO in 1992 illustrates this development at the European level. The concept of humanitarian interference, which was implemented under the aegis of the UN in three specific situations in Iraqi Kurdistan, the former Yugoslavia and Somalia, demonstrates that states have adopted the idea of non-governmental humanitarian action. At the same time, armed forces – instruments of the state – are being entrusted with humanitarian missions. Present during the acute phase of the crisis, they can be called upon to stay on when the crisis winds down (IFOR, followed by SFOR in the former Yugoslavia) and can even be entrusted with missions to set up the military component of certain peace accords (UNTAC in Cambodia, UNAVEM in Angola).

As humanitarian actors working in the same areas during the winding down phase of crises, we feel that it is important today to ponder the real, potential and desirable roles of armed forces during these rehabilitation periods. It is necessary to understand the context of the intervention of armed forces, its evolution and the influence of this evolution on the role devolved to the military in order to organise our thinking on the methods, means and objectives pursued by the different operators.

Military means for civilians

The civilian element that today constitutes the main concern in modern conflicts is at the core of the concepts of reconstruction and rehabilitation. Activities linked to restoring or consolidating peace are therefore primarily activities that are developed to benefit the civilian population. Demobilisation, de-mining in view of the return of refugees or displaced persons, the rebuilding of infrastructures, and the restoration of the rule of law through the training of police forces are all activities that rely on military capacities for the benefit of the civilian community. Armed forces have at their disposal considerable human and technical resources originally intended for military – or in the past few years military/humanitarian – intervention.

How do armed forces, states, and the major donors manage the military capacities at their disposal to respond to the specific needs of civil societies emerging from crises and undergoing a period of rehabilitation?

One actor among many

Managing the end of a crisis brings into the field a growing number of different actors. Conflict resolution requires various categories of interveners:

- the political and diplomatic bodies of various countries, whether they are members of a regional association or within the framework of an *ad hoc* group;
- humanitarian organisations, governmental or non-governmental;
- specialised agencies and their experts;
- private and institutional operators with an economic and financial objective.

How can the armed forces – themselves involved in the effort of the international community as a whole – coordinate their activities with those of the other actors?

An era of reduced military spending

The military present in the field develop a whole range of activities (including contracting, and the rebuilding of infrastructures) either spontaneously or within the framework of a general plan of action. For some armed forces, these activities hark back to a tradition of intervention that has its roots in colonisation. They are justified by the real needs of the population and by the means at the disposal of the troops in the field. As a part of their mandate, it is therefore even a duty for all the components of the international community to develop reconstruction and rehabilitation activities to help a country coming out of crisis. In the eyes of national public opinion, the image of soldiers as builders is reinforced by the media. How can the budgetary restrictions faced by Western armies since the collapse of the Communist bloc be dealt with in view of the increasing cost of reconstruction?

The logic of economics

The Americans have employed an offensive strategy to position themselves in order to pre-empt information and appeals for large international contracts. The privileged links that exist between the private sector and public bodies (such as USAID), and the uninterrupted and systematic flow of information between these sectors, partly explain the dominant part played by American industry in reconstruction operations in recent years.

The British base their strategy on the Department for International Development (formerly Overseas Development Assistance or ODA), the public cooperation agency of the Foreign Office, which is therefore directly linked to the political and economic policies of the government.

These two nations have already developed within their armed forces structures to put the latter in direct touch with their civilian environment, CIMIC for the Americans and Civil Affairs for the British, a concept that has been influential in the formulation of the UN structure. Germany and Japan, still mainly absent in military terms, have compensated for this by strategic management of their development aid to position themselves better economically at the end of crises.

This aspect of reconstruction and of the role devolved to national armed forces participating in multinational operations poses the problem of the underlying implications of a military presence in such situations. Are Western states trying, through their military presence, to conquer new market shares and profit from the dividends of peace?

Conclusion

In most cases, the signing of a peace accord does not mean that the crisis is over. The capacities of the state are profoundly affected, authority must be restored in a difficult context of a fragile balance of power, the economic situation is most often disastrous. In such a delicate context, reconstruction aid might appear as a factor of stabilisation and prevention, helping the country out of the cycle of violence.

The end of the crisis reveals new interlocutors at two levels. At the international level a government emerges seeking recognition and legitimacy; at the domestic level a new civil society appears. This crucial and complex phase in the evolution of a destabilised society certainly leaves room for a variety of interveners (state bodies such as diplomats and economic or military actors, and non-governmental organisations). The important question today is: are the objectives of all these actors compatible, and are their methods appropriate?

This is the context of the present study. The URD Group, in its capacity as a body of French non-governmental organisations that are present in the field in situations of emergency and rehabilitation, actively participates in the management of crises, and as interlocutors of the public authorities. As a participant, it calls into question the relevance of certain of these principles of action, and the role that armed forces should play in these situations.

Notes

1. The four Geneva Conventions of 1949 are binding on 188 states; 147 are party to Additional Protocol I, and 139 to Additional Protocol II.
2. Excepting bodies specialised in human rights or technical assistance for parliamentary mechanisms, such as the managers of the European Democracy Programme in countries eligible for PHARE and TACIS programmes.
3. The funding of these teams and of the methodological support (particularly from IRAM) was covered by the Fond d'aide et de coopération and the Caisse française de développement.
4. The matter of recapitalisation of livestock is among the most arduous. Even before the conflict heated up, livestock breeders were living in extremely precarious conditions, often with only a few head of cattle.
5. In the case of North Mali, five organisations of the Rhône-Alpes region of France signed a charter to coordinate their approach.

Epilogue

How difficult it is to formulate a common discourse for the NGOs, albeit on a matter that concerns them all: the relations between emergency and development practices. It is difficult because choosing to conduct reflection based on their respective experience draws on the very essence and history of each organisation. And it is difficult because the evolution of crises is not the subject of consensual analysis, and therefore results in different modes of intervention.

Consequently, it is not surprising that the opinions we have gathered are sometimes similar, often diverse and multi-faceted, or even contradictory. But the debate itself is shared by all. The many contributors we have brought together do not cover all the avenues for further debate. But they do demonstrate that it is possible, today, to get around institutional discourse, to go beyond outdated quarrels, and to debate the fundamental meaning and role of NGOs in international aid.

Indeed, it is clear that the debate does not stop at non-governmental circles. The donors, the political and administrative decision makers, the community leaders, and the representatives of international organisations – some of whom have recently staged symposia and encounters on this theme – are all confronted with the same questions. It is essential that the debates be extended to these bodies, and this is one of the goals of this work. But these institutions must expect to ponder their modes of political, military and financial intervention, and their administrative functioning – which is often too rigid and unable to respond to the complex problems we encounter today.

It is also clear that the debates must be extended to Southern and Eastern NGOs. The content of the idea of solidarity and its concrete forms of implementation will change in the coming years for at least two reasons:

◆ the ideology underlying the actions of Northern NGOs conveys universal values and is at the same time influenced by the Western cultures that have produced it;

◆ the traditional scenario of Northern NGOs going to the aid of partners in the South or the East who are working within their own cultures and on their own territories is becoming more intricate. Tomorrow, on the strength of their experience, NGOs from Burkina-Faso will go to the aid of Congo, Saudi NGOs may go to Algeria. We can be sure that that the cultural diversity of these non-governmental organisations will provide a fresh boost, new methods, and certainly some confrontations.

Finally, the debate is still open within the very organisations that have contributed to this work. Whether explicit or barely discernible, the questions they face are numerous and will have to be addressed.

◆◆◆

APPENDIX 1

An Analysis of Food Situations in a Crisis Context: East Kasaï, Zaïre

Marc Rodriguez

A description of the project, its objectives and its impact is offered in Part III.iii (pages 82–91). Criticism has been levelled at the omission of certain points of methodology which could have further improved the quality of the project. These points must be integrated into future projects if the experiences of the emergency and development specialists are to be combined successfully in the reinforcement of local capacities.

This criticism of the methodology touches essentially on five areas:
1. the conduct of initial analyses;
2. the methods for quantifying material support;
3. distribution criteria;
4. the blueprint for supply;
5. the versatility of a follow-up monitoring cell.

Although they were seasoned professionals (agronomists, economists, doctors), possessing the traditional diagnostic tools for assessing food situations or the state of health of a population, those who carried out the initial analyses in Kabinda hardly knew the area. Moreover, traditional methods of evaluation are hard to apply in a crisis situation. They make it possible to describe a situation at the time of the survey, but with a relatively high margin of uncertainty. They hardly explain its history or potential evolution. For interventions in the fields of health or food security, two elements are of prime importance in gauging the activities to be undertaken: the origins and destinations of the goods and health care outside the sphere of external intervention.

Conducting the initial analysis

At the start of an action, there are some unknowns in gauging the volume of aid that must be provided. One can only hypothesise about the attitude of the resident population towards the incoming population. Will the former continue to extend hospitality to the latter and, if so, according to what modalities and time frame? How will the market operate? Will supply spontaneously appear as a result of commercial activity, or will those who control supplies, if any, withhold them?

Rumours of renewed hostilities in Shaba have prompted fear of a new wave of migrants; but budget forecasts must be precise from the outset (for ECHO in particular). Integrating a new potential exodus – evaluating the number of people to be assisted – is difficult without reference figures.

Methods for quantifying existing local food capacity

Forecasting is difficult: a suitable method[1] consists of examining all the production systems for their capacity to yield a surplus in crisis situations and with respect to their harvesting schedule (detailed investigation of standing crops and granaries, identification of opportunities for remunerative farming or non-farming activities).

In the case of Kabinda, the forecasts were thwarted by events. Because of the hypothesis of a serious food shortage towards the end of the A Season (September 1994), a month of food supplies and distributions of seed and tools was planned to facilitate the rural integration of the refugees. Food distributions were overestimated because three points had been overlooked:

1. The assessment of food stocks of cassava. Subsequent studies of the production systems, notably by analysing the market for cassava in Mbudji Mayi, showed that these stocks represented a security margin of over six months.

2. The significance of Season B in the management of the stocks from Season A was underestimated. It appeared as though the farmers had held back their stocks, even to the point of tightening their belts during part of the B Season while waiting to be sure of the results of that season.[2] To this classic safety strategy were added commercial considerations as, little by little, through all sorts of income-generating activities, the refugees proved also to be clients.

3. The fact that the sub-region of Kabinda is located on a very important commercial route was not adequately considered. Quantities of grain and oil could have been mobilised for Kabinda to help cover the food shortage transit along this route.

There was no significant substantive difference in the diagnostic methodology of the emergency and development actors. Neither avoided the pitfalls of external surveys.

The debate on the standards of distribution

After several months, when uncertainty arose over the actual scale of the food shortage, it was decided that, rather than covering the whole of the hypothetical food shortage, basic rations would be reduced in the initial distributions to test the reaction of the population. The goal was to lessen destabilising effects on the market that might disrupt the economy of the resident population. But it took several weeks of angry debate between emergency and development actors to reach this wise decision because it upset the sacrosanct 'standards of distribution'.

It is not easy, moreover, for the managing institution to take such a decision, which entails a reduction in the running costs on which it can count to finance the general budget of its intervention. MSF, the manager designated by the European Union (to be replaced later by GRET), did not hesitate to take this decision.

The blueprint for supply

During the first six months, the MSF/GRET intervention in Kabinda was no different from those of the other agencies as far as the aim of the action was concerned:

♦ massive food distribution as of August, to bridge the gap;

♦ management of nutrition and health centres for the destitute.

An intervention that attempts to change the approach runs into two opposing ways of doing things: that of the emergency actors and that of the development actors.

Purchases of grain, oil and seeds posed the problem of choosing where to buy them, which to select, and the mode of transport.

Preoccupation with the harvest schedule prevailed and two serious studies were overlooked:

♦ on the capacity of modes of transport that could have been hired locally, for the transport to the villages as well;

♦ on the possibility of producing tools locally or in Mbudji Mayi or N'gandajika. The purchases were made in Kinshasa.

Finally, selected seeds have not proved, to date, any better than the local ones.

From the initial mission onwards, the logistics mechanism was set in motion and followed its own logic: the price of security, speed and the accomplishment of the declared goals was high. Although this reasoning may be justified in certain situations, it should not predominate, particularly as it introduces a primary mistrust *vis-à-vis* implementation by local operators.

Deficiencies of the follow-up monitoring process

Certainly, the monitoring worked well in that it made it possible to cancel in good time food distribution that had become useless and destabilising; to redirect activities towards a larger sector of the population; and to attain sooner the traditional objectives of the development phases. But the agronomists were too busy managing distribution. The follow-up monitoring was not done carefully enough, and did not accurately appraise the performance of the seeds that had been introduced or analyse the reference situation of the cultivated areas to measure the effect of the intervention on their cultivation. One had to make do with the general opinion of those concerned which, for that matter, was excellent.

Basically, the so-called emergency phase was important for the preparation of the second phase, entirely built on the relationship with the village development associations. It allowed the actors to get to know each other and, especially, to talk as much about the present as about the future.

In spite of the errors of method that have been described, the erratic rhythm of food distributions indubitably created a climate of trust and a certain ambience. This was to be very important for the remainder of the intervention: there was no latency interval between this period of survival and the structuring activities of a return to normal life. The momentum did not wane.

The list of inadequacies of the methods of this project could be summed up in one sentence: 'To improve resistance to compulsory figures in crisis situations.' It is agreed in emergency circles that in this type of situation, food aid, selected seeds and tools must be brought in. It is a hard-and-fast rule, particularly for the donors. To refuse to comply would be to take the risk of being neither understood, nor followed.

APPENDIX 2
The European Union and Support for Rehabilitation
XAVIER ORTÉGAT AND SYLVIE MANTRANT

On 22 November 1996, the Council passed a regulation concerning rehabilitation and reconstruction actions on behalf of developing countries. Support for rehabilitation is thus henceforth an integral part of the tools at the disposal of the Union in the framework of its relations with developing countries. This type of assistance supplements the other two more traditional types of aid: humanitarian aid and development cooperation. But the nature of this new tool requires clarification because rehabilitation does not fit into a defined space – between the other two forms of aid – which has just been discovered and needs to be filled. What follows shows that clarification does not necessarily lead to a definition – at least in the present case – because the content of support for rehabilitation and the forms it may take bring to light the possibility of recourse to a variety of open and adaptable approaches rather than identifying a limited framework for operations.

In December 1995, the Madrid Declaration adopted at the Humanitarian Summit had launched an appeal to the international community for

> resources to remain available to meet the challenge of rebuilding war-shattered societies and thus consolidate a peace settlement and prevent the seeds of future disaster from being sown. The links between relief and development must be strengthened and local capacity to cope must be reinforced. Reconstruction involves not only water systems, bridges and roads but also civil society: the demobilisation of soldiers and the rebuilding of the judiciary and administration and of education and social services. Flexible mechanisms to provide more funding for emergency rehabilitation must be found. At the same time, relief must be managed efficiently in order to phase out humanitarian aid as soon as the emergency period is over, switching over rapidly to other forms of assistance.

The Declaration followed an announcement by the Commission to the European Parliament and the Council on 12 May 1993, concerning a special support programme for rehabilitation in developing countries that would bring to the fore the specificity and importance of the need for aid for rehabilitation and reconstruction in developing countries that have suffered serious destruction due to war, civil strife or natural disasters.

Is finding a definition really necessary?

The Madrid Declaration referred to 'emergency rehabilitation', which limited

164

somewhat the scope of the instrument. This limitation, moreover, could appear to contradict the principal objective of rehabilitation aid: reconstruction aimed at durability. In this respect, the previously mentioned regulation specifies the content of rehabilitation actions: they aim to help rebuild the functioning of the economy and the institutional capacities necessary to restore the social and political stability of the countries concerned and fulfil the needs of all the affected populations. They must take over progressively from humanitarian action and prepare for the resumption of development aid in the middle and long terms.

The regulation identifies two objectives: the return to a situation that permits functioning and management as well as durability. Another element also appears: to establish a link between two situations – in other words, to go beyond straightforward emergency relief and aim for results in the long term, ensuring a transition.

But what type of transition? Creating a link between emergency aid, reha-bilitation and development can be justified by the identification of a specific area which corresponds neither to emergency relief nor to development coop-eration. The statement of the Commission of 28 March 1996 indeed empha-sises that disasters are costly both in terms of human lives and resources; that they disrupt economic and social development; that they require long periods of rehabilitation and give rise to distinct bureaucratic structures and proce-dures that duplicate the role of the institutions specialised in development. At the same time, development policy only too often ignores the risk of drought or other traumas, as well as the fact that it is necessary to protect vulnerable families by helping them perfect strategies of self-defence. Creating a link between emergency aid and development will make it possible to lessen these deficiencies, according to the statement. But the same announcement goes on to indicate an important reservation, saying that this simple model does not sufficiently take into account the realities of many emergency situations. Most of these situations are not due to natural disasters but proceed from a combi-nation of several forms of political, economic and social instability that are often the result of errors of management, the failure of economic policies and the inadequacy of development programmes that have exacerbated ethnic or religious differences. The idea that emergency aid leads, via rehabilitation, to long-term development discounts the chronic nature of many disaster situations.

Debating the much-vaunted emergency–rehabilitation–development con-inuum is therefore perhaps not the best way to define rehabilitation in terms of space, time and practices. And this is the problem with summing up rehabili-tation as whatever is not humanitarian action or development aid. This is the problem with defining rehabilitation in relation to other forms of aid and not by its own specificity.

And what is more, although rehabilitation aid does not necessarily come between emergency aid and the resumption of development, it is strictly speaking neither emergency aid nor development aid, in that it attempts to provide both a rapid response to the crisis and sustainable solutions. Perhaps, therefore, the question should be approached from another angle. Indeed, if one concentrates on the above-mentioned characteristics – reconstruction, transition and sustainability – the diversity and range of rehabilitation interventions become clear.

Variable and adaptable interventions

In fact, the idea of rehabilitation aid covers a variety of approaches, fields and moments of intervention. These are linked to the identification, in a given situation, of the various needs that crop up at different stages of the intervention, or simultaneously. Moreover, they are linked to the potentialities of each situation and how to adapt to them. This is what makes rehabilitation aid difficult to define – but then, is it really necessary to define it?

To be convinced of this, one has only to refer again to the regulation of the Council, which sets down the fields in which rehabilitation actions can be undertaken as: quick-starting a sustainable production system; material and functional rehabilitation of basic infrastructures, including de-mining; social reintegration, particularly for refugees, displaced persons and demobilised military personnel; and the restoration of the institutional capacities necessary to the rehabilitation phase, particularly at the local level. There are, actually, important differences in practice and approach between a procedure that tackles the reconstruction of basic infrastructures – an operation that can be carried out relatively quickly – and one that favours social reintegration, which requires considerable means, very accurate social, political, and economic analysis, and long-term planning.

These regulations seem to indicate that there are several forms of rehabilitation that can be undertaken as soon as we are faced with an emergency situation. Beyond determining whether these forms of rehabilitation address the short or the long term and are called 'emergency rehabilitation' or just 'rehabilitation', it is probably most important to identify the specificity of rehabilitation aid and the situations in which it can be implemented.

The specificity of rehabilitation

Research on the specificity of rehabilitation is still a trial and error process. But although we are trying to find the answers, we recommend that the considerations discussed below be taken into account.

Complementarity

The fact that rehabilitation aid overlaps with but does not cover more traditional forms of aid might imply that it is a complementary approach that has benefited from the lessons of emergency and development aid, and enriches them. But how does it enrich them? Taking up the matter of complementarity means taking into account a serious problem: the fact that most donors make an institutional distinction between emergency and development.

Prevention

The Madrid Declaration states that we must prevent the seeds of future disaster from being sown. This means that preventive action and, to a lesser extent, disaster preparedness are an integral part of this approach to humanitarian aid. But disaster prevention is difficult to implement and, above all, it requires context analysis in order to predict potential conflicts. At this stage it seems that, on the one hand, the involvement of local actors is essential and, on the other, that evaluation of impact on the renewal of intervention models and practices is necessary.

Taking the context into account

The Madrid Declaration often mentions rehabilitation in the context of the reconstruction of war-shattered societies. Certainly, this emphasis reflects the present trend of humanitarian crises, which are increasingly taking place in situations of war or tension, mainly linked to internal conflicts. On the one hand, it is in this new context that traditional forms of international aid appear most inadequate; on the other, it is in contexts of fragmented, sometimes endemic violence that the limits of emergency aid are most cruelly felt. When development cannot be envisaged, and when repeated emergency action is not enough, endemic and chronic crisis calls not only for rehabilitation, but also for the building of new capacities to enable the population and social structures to cope with the crisis and face the risks.

Essential steps towards rehabilitation aid: identifying the potentialities

Although rehabilitation aid represents a new form of assistance that addresses the complexities of humanitarian situations, it cannot be univocal. Furthermore, it does not substitute for emergency or development aid but, as we have seen, is complementary in several ways:

- by deploying activities that belong neither to emergency aid nor to development projects;
- possibly by ensuring a transition that begins with emergency and simultaneously contributes to the resumption of development;
- by introducing a new perspective, both in the emergency and in the development phase.

This new perspective stems precisely from the fact that rehabilitation activities are many and are determined according to the type of crisis or disaster they attempt to address. Depending on whether the humanitarian crisis is linked to a natural disaster or a conflict, and on the level of development and the culture of the country in which it takes place, the responses in terms of rehabilitation are obviously variable. This variability is a fundamental aspect of rehabilitation activities. Therein lies their major advantage: theirs is an approach that is open to change, that even favours it.

♦ They improve existing structures in the reconstruction phase. The idea is not to replicate exactly that which existed (which could lead to reproducing previous errors and thus to a new crisis). Rehabilitation thus becomes modernisation and renovation to prevent the recurrence of crises.

♦ They encourage reform to reduce risks and build up the capacities of the local population.

♦ They foster social inventiveness to appease tensions in post-conflict situations.

Rehabilitation activities stimulate analysis and a better understanding of the evolution of the societies in which they are implemented. The variability of the solutions to be provided means that these activities must be flexible and adaptable to very different realities. They should not be set according to a strict model of intervention but should take into account the complexity of human situations, which implies dialogue and consultation with the local population. Furthermore, rehabilitation plays a complementary role to emergency relief and development cooperation. In this respect, the development of global planning strategies that include heightened coordination between the actors improves this complementarity. Finally, the concerns it encompasses, in particular acting on the causes of conflicts to reduce the frequency of humanitarian crises, lead to a very wide range of economic, political, social and cultural activities.

Looking to the future

Among the many obvious provisional conclusions, one stands out. Rehabilitation aid introduces a new perspective that makes it possible to deal more adequately with the needs arising from crisis situations: this is the link between rehabilitation and capacity building. Rehabilitation aid does not lead to a return to normal; the idea is not to rebuild identical structures but to offer populations and societies the possibility of life in new and better conditions and to better protect themselves against the risks that surround them – as we have seen, this means renovating, modernising, encouraging reform and preparing for the future. Faced with complex emergencies, this capacity-building process enables the development of long-term and therefore necessarily participatory action. This process is then a factor of discovery and identification of the evolution of a society and/or a given situation.

It is probably in this sense that rehabilitation aid can enrich the other two forms of aid: by anticipating and reacting to tensions, on the one hand, and, on the other, by analysing global frameworks for reconstruction that integrate the specific and new factors of development: economic, social and political.

APPENDIX 3

A History of the Partnership between the ICRC and the National Red Cross and Red Crescent Societies

Carlo von Flüe

In 1859, faced with the horror of seeing thousands of wounded soldiers abandoned to their fate, a Geneva citizen named Henri Dunant improvised aid to the victims, using the meagre resources he had at hand. This act of human solidarity gave rise to the idea of making preparations in peacetime to ensure that the woefully inadequate army medical services of the day would not be all there was when war came. Volunteers would be trained and their neutral status on the battlefield guaranteed so that they could assist all the wounded impartially.

An organisation was needed specifically for this activity, and the 'International Committee for Relief to Wounded Soldiers' – the future International Committee of the Red Cross (ICRC) – thus saw the light of day. National governments then had to be won over to the idea that the wounded soldiers from the other side and those who cared for them should not be regarded as enemies, and that since they were not, or no longer, taking part in the fighting, they were entitled to protection. Hence came the idea of an international treaty that among other things would enshrine a protective emblem to be used by all armies to identify, in the same manner, their medical personnel, vehicles and establishments.

The International Committee began in October 1863 by convening experts from 16 countries. They adopted ten resolutions of what amounted to the founding charter of the Red Cross, setting out as it did the tasks and working methods of the proposed committees for relief to the wounded, to be established in each country.

At a diplomatic conference the following year, twelve states signed the *Convention for the Amelioration of the Condition of the Wounded in Armies in the Field*, the first Geneva Convention. Law would henceforth play a role in the midst of war by laying down rules for the comportment of the combatants. Ever since, the treaties constituting international humanitarian law have grown in number and been regularly updated.

The International Red Cross and Red Crescent Movement

The Movement today is composed of the ICRC (its founding body), the various National Red Cross and Red Crescent Societies and their International

Federation, established in 1919, which supports the National Societies' activities for the benefit of vulnerable groups within the population.

With its headquarters in Geneva, the ICRC acts – on its own initiative or on the basis of the 1949 Geneva Conventions and their Additional Protocols of 1977 – as a neutral intermediary between parties to conflict, providing impartial protection and assistance to the victims of armed conflict or of other situations marked by violence.

The ICRC, the National Societies and their International Federation are independent entities. They have their own statutes and none of them exercises any authority over the others. It is nevertheless the ICRC, in its capacity as guardian of the Movement's fundamental principles, that verifies whether future National Societies will be able to carry out their activities in accordance with those principles and, if such is the case, officially recognises them. This recognition makes them full members of the international Movement and entitles them to apply for membership of the Federation.

The National Red Cross and Red Crescent Societies

The National Red Cross and Red Crescent Societies were originally set up to work side by side with the military medical services in caring for wounded and sick soldiers. Today they perform a multitude of activities in peacetime as well.

The National Societies are authorised to use the red cross or red crescent emblem in accordance both with national legislation governing its 'use as an indicative device' and with regulations adopted by the entire Movement in conjunction with the states party to the Geneva Conventions.

The National Societies undertake to use the emblem only in connection with activities that are in keeping with the Movement's seven fundamental principles. The emblem's use as an indicative device identifies individuals and objects as being affiliated with the Movement. Its use 'as a protective device' identifies individuals and objects that may not be attacked in the event of armed conflict.

Each state party to the Geneva Conventions has the obligation at all times to prevent and punish any use of the emblem not expressly authorised by the 1949 Geneva Conventions and their Additional Protocols of 1977.

APPENDIX 4
The Fundamental Principles of the International Red Cross and Red Crescent Movement

The fundamental principles do not each have the same value, but what is important is the way they fit together, becoming the common denominator for all components of the International Red Cross and Red Crescent Movement, the foundation for its policy. Applying them requires a good understanding of their scope; each of the Movement's components is responsible for this. It is different with international humanitarian law, responsibility for the implementation of which lies with the states.

The fundamental principles were reaffirmed at the 25th International Conference of the Red Cross and Red Crescent in 1986, when they were incorporated in the Movement's Statutes. They enshrine the Movement's identity and specific nature and guide it in its approach. There are at present seven principles.

Humanity

The International Red Cross and Red Crescent Movement, born of a desire to bring assistance without discrimination to the wounded on the battlefield, endeavours, in its international and national capacities, to prevent and alleviate human suffering wherever it may be found. Its purpose is to protect life and health and to ensure respect for the human being. It promotes mutual understanding, friendship, cooperation and lasting peace amongst all peoples.

Impartiality

The Movement makes no discrimination as to nationality, race, religious beliefs, class or political opinions. It endeavours to relieve the suffering of individuals, being guided solely by their needs, and to give priority to the most urgent cases of distress.

Neutrality

In order to continue to enjoy the confidence of all, the Movement may not take sides in hostilities or engage at any time in controversies of a political, racial, religious or ideological nature.

Independence

The Movement is independent. The National Societies, while auxiliaries in the humanitarian services of their governments and subject to the laws of their respective countries, must always maintain their autonomy so that they may be able at all times to act in accordance with the principles of the Movement.

Voluntary Service

The Red Cross and Red Crescent is a voluntary relief movement not prompted in any manner by desire for gain.

Unity

There can be only one Red Cross or one Red Crescent Society in any one country. It must be open to all. It must carry on its humanitarian activities throughout its territory.

Universality

The International Red Cross and Red Crescent Movement, in which all Societies have equal status and share equal responsibilities and duties in helping each other, is world-wide.

APPENDIX 5
Emergency Food Aid
Marie Cécile Thirion and François Grunewald

Emergency food aid represents annually between three and four million tonnes of food supplies, managed mainly by NGOs and international organisations. Its principal objective is to save lives endangered by the destructuring, or even destruction of the mechanisms of production, marketing, access to food, or by the displacement of populations.

The scale of the operations and the diversity of situations in the field have given emergency operators and logisticians occasion to assert their skills: quick delivery in difficult situations, the organisation of distribution, the setting up of feeding centres in the most serious cases. But this mode of management tends to mask the evolution of the context in which the operation takes place and the assessment of its impact on future development.

The developers propose a different interpretation of these situations while aiming at the same results.

Where diagnosis is concerned

A food crisis, more than a matter of nutrition, is first and foremost a problem of decapitalisation and of the loss of access to food. The tools developed by emergency operators focus heavily on anthropometric indicators. Experience shows that, in most cases, socio-economic analysis of the dynamics of loss of access (progressive or rapid) to food is much more relevant both for predicting and intervening, thereby limiting the extent of the disaster. The methods of rapid evaluation and the analysis of rural and urban micro-economics prove to be powerful diagnostic tools for food crises and hence for the decision-making process.

A broader analysis of the context of the crisis

Development NGOs have long supported local and regional purchasing as a means of supporting local production and markets. In times of crisis this approach is all the more appropriate as it is a matter of participating in rebuilding production, economic, and social structures. Yet, no matter what the scale of the crisis, we observe that there generally are markets that continue to function, or quickly resume their activity, if not at the local level, then at least at the regional level (Sudan, Somalia). The setting up of a simple system to monitor these phenomena has made it possible to evaluate when and where purchases could be made locally. It also makes it possible to supply food that is adapted to local dietary habits, and in many cases (for example in countries that are isolated) to supply it more rapidly.

To support these markets that are often weakened by crisis, systems must rapidly be deployed to monitor prices, supply and production, as organisations are often faced with problems of availability (low volume of goods on the market), quality, and reliability of operators and of transport. Hence the importance of in-depth and up-to-date knowledge of the market mechanisms – all the more so as poor management of local purchasing can destabilise the market by generating speculation and price hikes, and their consequences for the poorest consumers. This was the case when the WFP and NGOs in Uganda organised the purchase of massive quantities of beans for the Rwandan refugees.

Integrating food aid operations to reinforce food security

Food aid is but one of the components to reactivate production and marketing and not a univocal and global solution. To achieve this aim, the aid must be part of a reorganisation and reinforcement of the existing social structures that are indispensable to long-term development. This implies a participatory commitment on the part of the beneficiary individuals and structures. Identifying these structures is a delicate matter, especially after man-made crises. However, the beneficiaries must be included as early as possible in the different stages of the operations (assessment of needs, implementation and follow-up of actions, monitoring of the results). The aim should be to avoid further decapitalisation of the population, so that it can preserve its tools of production and thus resume its activities after the crisis. Thus food aid allows the beneficiaries to keep their livestock, their production tools and their seeds rather than selling them to buy food.

Finally, it is a reflex of development actors to organise as soon as possible the follow-up of their actions. It is not just a matter of determining who has received what, but of assessing the part played by food aid in the revival of production and consumption. Only a keen understanding of these complex situations will make it possible to structure effectively the various stages leading up to the discontinuation of food distributions.

As we see all too often, food crises recur in the same spots where food aid has been provided, indicating the inadequacy of purely substitutive food aid that is not part of a long-term process.

174

BIBLIOGRAPHY

Adams, Mark, and Mark Bradbury (1996) 'Conflict and Development'. OXFAM Discussion Paper No. 4, OXFAM.

Agency for Cooperation and Research in Development (ACORD) (1993) 'Être opérationnel dans la turbulence'. Document, February.

Anderson, M., *et al.* (1989) *Rising From the Ashes: Development Strategies in Times of Disaster*. UNESCO.

Bennett, Jon and Mary Kayitesi-Blewitt (1996) *Comprendre le conflit et construire la paix*. CODEP, December.

Brauman, Rony (1994) *Devant le mal: Rwanda, un génocide en direct*. Arléa.

Brauman, Rony (1995) *L'action humanitaire*. Flammarion.

Brauman, Rony (1996) *Humanitaire le dilemne. Conversations pour demain avec Philippe Petit*. Textuel.

Centre de Recherche et d'Action Social (CERAS) (1994) 'L'humanitaire sans frontières'. *Projet* (CERAS quarterly).

Centre international d'études pour le développement local (CIEDEL) (1993–5) 'Du bricolage au développement'; 'Synergie entre acteurs'; 'Culture de guerre culture de paix'; 'Développement panne de sens'. *Histoires de développement*, Nos 15, 21, 26, 31.

Centre internationale de recherche agronomique pour le développement (CIRAD) (1985) 'Le suivi et l'évaluation de projets de développement rural'. *Les cahiers de la recherche/développement*, No. 5, Montpellier.

Comité catholique contre la faim et pour le développement (CCFD) (annual) *Le baromètre de la solidarité internationale des français*.

Comité de liaison des organisations non-gouvernementales de développement (CLONGD) (1994) *Conflits, développement et interventions militaires: rôles, positions et expériences des ONG*. April.

Comité français de solidarité internationale (CFSI) (1994) Synthesis Report on the Symposium on Emergency–Rehabilitation–Development, Arche de la Défense, November.

Comité pour les technologies appropriées (COTA) (1994) *Evaluation des actions financées sur la ligne budgétaire Réhabilitation (//5071) Afrique australe*. Report drafted for the European Commission, Brussels.

Commission Coopération Développement (1994) *Evaluer pour évoluer: compte rendu de la table ronde*. Paris.

Croissance (1997) 'De la décolonisation à la mondialisation, la longue marche d'un journal pour le développement'. No. 400 (January).

Cultures et conflits (1993) 'Interventions armées et causes humanitaires'. No. 11. L'Harmattan.

Department of Humanitarian Affairs of the United Nations (DHA) (1995) 'Building Local Capacity and Strengthening Coping Mechanisms in the Context of Relief and Development. Some Challenges for the International Community'. Discussion paper, ECOSOC/DHA.

Destexhe, Alain (1993) *L'humanitaire impossible ou deux siècles d'ambiguité*. Armand Colin.

Eriksson, John (1996) *The International Response to Conflict and Genocide: Lessons from the Rwanda Experience*. Synthesis report, Steering Committee of the Joint Evaluation of Emergency Assistance to Rwanda, March.

Esprit (1994) 'Pour une solitude plurielle'. July.

European Commission (1993) *Manuel de gestion du cycle de projet: approche intégrée et cadre logique*.

European Commission (1996) *Evaluation des projets de recherche et de développement technologique: propositions techniques. Tender VIII/A/FD/cv/4-7-1996*, Evaluation Department, Brussels.

European Union (1993) *Programme spécial d'appui à la réhabilitation dans les pays en développement*. Communication of the Commission to the European Parliament, 12 May.

European Union (1995) *Les liens entre l'urgence, la réhabilitation et le développement (LRRD), Historique, conclusions et recommendations*. November.

European Union (1996) Communication of the Commission to the European Parliament, 28 March.

European Union (1996) *Règlement (CE) No. 2258/96 du Conseil, relatif à des actions de réhabilitation et de reconstruction en faveur des pays en développement*. 22 November.

Fondation pour le Progès de l'Homme (1996) *Journée de travail sur la prévention des conflits*. Atelier du Sud, 2 December.

Grunewald, François (1989) *Alarme précoce, urgence et développement: quelques idées pour une stratégie*. Asian Disaster Preparedness Centre, Bangkok.

Grunewald, François (1995) 'From Prevention to Rehabilitation. Before, During and After: the ICRC in Retrospect'. *International Review of the Red Cross*, No. 306 (May–June).

Grunewald, François (1997) *Au-delà de la survie. Concepts et pratiques de réhabilitation*. Division des secours, International Committee of the Red Cross (ICRC), January.

Hagman, G. (1988) 'Des secours en cas de désastre au développement', *Revue Internationale de la Croix Rouge*, No. 771 (May).

Hagman, G. (1988) *From Diasaster Relief to Development*. HDI Studies on Development, No. 1. Henry Dunant Institute.

Husson, Bernard (1995) *L'humanitaire, une manifestation de la montée de l'individualisme*. CIEDEL, November.

Institut d'études de développement (IEDES) (1969) *Guide d'évaluation économique et financière des projets*. Ministry of Cooperation, Paris.

Institut universitaire des études de développement (IUED) (1996), *Le système de programmation – suivi – évaluation dans une démarche institutionnelle*. Geneva.

Institute of Development Studies (IDS) (1994) 'Linking Relief and Development', *IDS Bulletin*, Vol. 25, No. 4 (October), University of Sussex, Brighton.

International Committee of the Voluntary Agencies (ICVA) (1995) *A Symposium on the Role of NGO Emergency Assistance in Promoting Peace and Reconciliation*. March.

International Federation of Red Cross and Red Crescent Societies (IFRC) (1993) *Disaster Needs Assessment*. Manual, IFRC.

Jean, François, and Jean-Christophe Ruffin (eds) (1996) *Economie des guerres civiles*. Hachette.

Kiefer, G., (1995) *Echo Operation Manual for the Evaluation of International Aid*. European Commission on Humanitarian Operations (ECHO).

Lautze, S. (1996) 'Lives versus Livelihood: How to Foster Self-Sufficiency and Productivity of Disaster Victims'. Occasional paper, ODA/USAID.

Lautze, S. (1996) *Coping with Crisis, Coping with Aid: Capacity Building, Coping Mechanisms and Dependency, Linking Relief and Development. An Analysis Prepared for the UN Inter-Agency Sub-Working Group*. International Famine Center, Tufts University.

McCrae, Joanna, and Anthony Zwi, with Vivienne Forsythe (1995) *Post-Conflict Rehabilitation:*

Preliminary Issues for Consideration by the Health Sector. London School of Hygiene and Tropical Medicine.

Médecins sans frontières (MSF) (1992–) *Populations en danger* and *Face aux crises*. Yearly updates since 1992, Pluriel and La Découverte.

Médecins sans frontières (MSF) (1996) *Mini Symposium on Evaluation and Impact Studies of Humanitarian Relief Intervention: Final Report*. Amsterdam.

Netherlands Development Cooperation (1994) *Humanitarian Aid to Somalia*. Operation Review Unit, Netherlands Development Cooperation.

Organisation for Economic Cooperation and Development (OECD) (1996) *Une étude par pays sur les relations des ONG et des pouvoirs publics*. Development Aid Committee, OECD.

Overseas Development Institute (ODI) (1995) *Aid Under Fire: Redefining Relief and Development Assistance in Unstable Conditions*. ODI, April.

OXFAM (1991) *Social Survey Method: a Field Guide for Development Workers*. Development Guidelines, No. 6, Oxford.

Perrot, Marie-Dominique (ed.) (1994) *Dérives humanitaires*. Nouveaux cahiers, IUED, April.

Reynaud, Jean-François and Bruno Rebelle (eds) (1995) *Développement en crises*. Vétérinaires sans frontières (VSF) 1995.

Royal Ministry of Foreign Affairs of Norway (1993) *Evaluation of Development Assistance: Handbook for Evaluators and Managers*. Oslo.

Ruffin, Jean-Christophe (1992) *L'aventure humanitaire*. Gallimard.

Ruffin, Jean-Christophe (1992) *Le piège humanitaire*. Hachette.

Smith, Stephen (1993) *Somalie. La guerre perdue de l'humanitaire*. Calmann Lévy.

Solidarités agricoles et alimentaires (SOLAGRAL) (1995) 'Aide d'urgence, les ONG au front'. *Courrier de la planète*, No. 27 (April).

Solidarités agricoles et alimentaires (SOLAGRAL)/Comité français de solidarité internationale (CFSI) (1995) *L'enjeu alimentaire dans le continuum urgence, réhabilitation, développement*. Symposium organised by the French Development NGOs Platform, Paris, 16 May.

Tsikounas, Myriam (ed.) (1996) *Les ambiguités de l'humanitaire: de Saint Vincent de Paul aux French Doctors*. Le Seuil.

Urgence–Réhabilitation–Développement (URD) (1995) *URD Newsletter* (ed. Claire Pirotte), June.

Vuianovitch, Danielle (1993) *Urgence et développement; une phase intermédiaire: la réhabilitation*. Comité français de solidarité internationale (CFSI), April.

World Food Programme (WFP) (1996) 'Experience in Strengthening Local Capacity and Coping Mechanisms and Encouraging Transition from Relief to Development'. Paper presented to the ECOSOC Taskforce of the IASC Sub-Working Group on Local Capacity, Geneva.

INDEX

178

Cross/Crescent movement 95-6; principles of 90-1
Peru 12, 118, 143-4
PHARE (Aid for the Economic Reconstruction of Poland and Hungary) 54, 157n
Poland 123
political constraints 62-4
population 19, 42, 58, 76
Portugal 16
privatisation 148
process vs project 71
professionalisation of aid *xix, xxi*, 5, 70
progress myth 19

quasi-states *xv*
Quechua 144
Quick Impact Projects 53

Rakhine state 110-11
Reagan, President 16
reconciliation 121, 132-3, 145-6
reconstruction, economic 60, 67, 145-6, 107, 148, 156, 165-6, 173-4; industrial 60, 107; social 138, 164-8, 173-4
Red Crescent movement 95-6, 128, 169-72; National Societies 95-6, 169-70
Red Cross movement 95-6, 128, 169-72; National Societies 95-6, 169-70; *see also* International Committee of the Red Cross (ICRC)
refugees *xiv*, 5, 25, 40, 50, 54, 58, 83-4, 87, 98, 106, 110-11, 125, 147-8, 154, 160-1, 166, 174
rehabilitation 36-41, 44-6, 49-56, 60, 85, 99, 101, 129, 138, 141, 145-6, 148, 154-5, 164-8
Relief Society of Tigray *xiii*
religion 84, 125
religious fundamentalism 7, 99
Rescue the Nomads 59
research-development 114
road making 51, 53, 86, 107, 110
Rocard, Michel 70
Rohingyas 110-11
Russia 6
Rwanda *xiv, xvi*, 2-3, 6, 14, 27, 77, 118, 124, 127, 129-30, 132-3, 174
Rwandan Popular Forces (RPF) *xvi-xvii*, 129, 132-3

Sahel 42, 74
Salam operation 81
sanctions 124
sanitation *xviii*, 51, 92, 111, 118, 151

Santo Domingo 15
Saudi Arabia 159
Scandinavia *xix*
Second World War 15, 46
Secours et assistance médicale d'urgence (SAMU) 10
self-reliance 68, 84-6
Senegal
Serbia *xvi*
Shaba region 83-5, 160
shelter 29, 32, 44, 50
Shining Path (SP) 143-4
SIDKA syndicate 86-7
Sierra Leone 2, 6, 73
social organisation 44, 74, 80, 90, 108, 113, 134, 137, 149, 166-7
solidarity *xvii, xxi-xxii*, 1, 5, 21, 26, 28, 49, 53, 55, 62, 64, 68-9, 80-1, 124, 130, 153, 158-9, 169
Somalia *xiv-xv*, 2, 12, 20, 45, 55, 58, 64, 68, 81, 91, 98-9, 105-6, 118, 130, 154, 173
Somoza regime 16
Songhié 86
South America 6
Southern African Development Community (SADC) 3
Soviet Union (former) 15-16, 104, 138
Spanish Sahara 16
Special Force for Bosnia Herzegovina (SFOR) 154
speculation 24, 105, 174
SPHERE *xviii*, 5-6
Sri Lanka 16
standards *xviii, xxi*, 5-6, 161
state humanitarian aid 150-1, 154-6
state–NGO relationship *xix-xx*, 6, 21, 62-3, 113, 137-8, 151, 156, 158
substitution practices 35, 44, 46, 48, 51-2, 54, 71, 153
Sudan *xvi, xxi*, 3, 7, 20, 73, 110, 173
sustainability *xxii*, 52, 54, 63, 67, 71, 90, 103, 114, 166

Taliban 139
Technical Assistance to the Community of Independent States (TACIS) 105, 157n
Thailand 50, 54
Third World 15-16
Tibet 74, 110-11
Tibeto-Burmans 74, 110-11
Timbuktu 39, 145
tontines 73
trade 44, 106, 148
trade unions 81, 91
training 38, 44, 48, 54, 67, 70, 92, 107,